Artificial Intelligence, Machine Learning and Big Data

Beginner's guide to Artificial Intelligence, Machine Learning, Big Data and its application

Robin Paul

professional advice. The content within this book has been derived from various sources. Please consult a licensed professional before attempting any techniques outlined in this book.

By reading this document, the reader agrees that under no circumstances is the author responsible for any losses, direct or indirect, that are incurred as a result of the use of the information contained within this document, including, but not limited to, errors, omissions, or inaccuracies.

Table of Contents

Introduction

As we step into the Fourth Industrial Revolution, there are new buzzwords that dominate conversations. These buzzwords include 'Artificial Intelligence,' 'AI,' 'machine learning' and 'Big Data.' We use these words in much the same way an elite person shows their VIP ticket. There's an aura of "Of course I know what these terms are!" But, do they? And when you think about it, do *you* know what these terms mean?

You probably have a rough idea of what these terms mean, but, if you don't, there's no need to worry. I wrote this book with an absolute novice in mind, so irrespective of your level of understanding you should find this book informative. These systems — whether used in tandem or together — will work exceptionally well in a variety of industries. Currently, AI is dominating the commercial sector. We are seeing these AI and Big Data systems being used voraciously to improve business and customer relations. As a member of the public, understanding how businesses will use your data is important because it will allow you to make informed decisions about the usage of your data. Being knowledgeable about how your data is used also keeps you from being subconsciously sucked into consuming more than you need.

Unfortunately, if you are a computer scientist or AI specialist, then this book will prove to be lacking. It does not dive into all the gorgeous technicalities of AI, but it might very well give you nostalgia as we go through the highlights of AI's journey. If you're looking for a way to explain AI to any of your non-technical friends or family, then this book may give you the words to explain these terms without getting too technical and losing them.

We are keeping things simple, so there are only four chapters in this book. Each chapter begins with a brief explanation of what the term is before explaining the various components that make it up. Once we understand what each topic breaks down into, we then take a tour through the history of it. This will help you to understand the progress, and gain an appreciation for the advancements that have occurred and will occur. Lastly, we look at several ways that these systems add value to our lives or will add value to them in the future. I will also provide a list of places that you can look at if you are interested in going to the field as well as various jobs that may interest you.

To illustrate this, I will be using the chapter on artificial intelligence — the term is explained and then the various components that comprise AI are discussed. AI is an umbrella term, so when we speak about AI, it's about as broad as speaking about berries — there are many types of berries and each is different. Once you understand the various components of AI, then I will take you on a tour of

AI's history. Did you know AI is only 70-odd years old? It's one of the youngest yet fastest advancing science fields that we have. It is important to understand the history of AI so that you can fully appreciate the benefits of using AI and understand the impact it will have on the future.

In the last chapter, I will look at how machine learning, Big Data, and AI can be used together. However, I will also delve into the ethical issues that the use of these systems raises. You should understand that even though these advances are extraordinary and have the potential to change lives, there is also the potential to wreak havoc.

Ultimately, I want to teach you about the wonderful world of artificial intelligence, machine learning, and Big Data. I want you to understand what it is and the impact that it will have on all future endeavors. Hopefully, after reading this book you will be inspired to learn more about AI, machine learning, and Big Data. Given that we need specialists in this field because of the current boom in the industry: it would give me immense pleasure to know that this book inspired you to pursue a career in computer science and specialize in any of these components.

Now let's go forth and explore!

"We've never seen a technology move as fast as AI has to impact society and technology. This is by far the fastest-moving technology that we've ever tracked in terms of its impact and we're just getting started." — Paul Daugherty

Chapter 1: What is Artificial Intelligence?

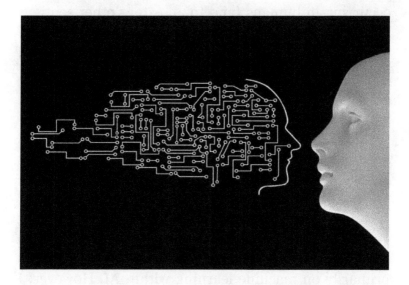

Welcome to the beautiful world of Artificial Intelligence (AI). I'm sure you've heard the term 'AI' or 'Artificial Intelligence' irrespective of what field you're in. With the advent of the Fourth Industrial Revolution, AI has taken the world by storm. In the simplest terms, AI is a branch of computer science that attempts to recreate the natural intelligence of humans. While that definition is extremely broad — it is apt because AI is an immense field with many sub-fields. So, to build on your understanding of AI, you must understand the 'big idea' of AI: it [AI] is an attempt to recreate human intelligence, and to understand AI, you must look at what artificial intelligence is in relation to human intelligence (Raj Ramesh, 2017).

'Artificial intelligence' already tells you that this is an attempt to recreate the intelligence that is naturally occurring in humans (and to an extent other sentient beings), but this notion forces you to reevaluate your understanding of intelligence. What constitutes intelligence? How do we define it? Is it just knowing a lot of information? These are all questions that have been asked through the years. Once you understand the different types of AI and how they work, you will see how the understanding of intelligence constantly changed and influenced the AI systems that were created.

We can break AI into two subsections: machine learning and symbolic learning. This book will focus primarily on machine learning within AI. However, I will explain symbolic learning and its components so that you have a thorough understanding of everything that AI encompasses. Artificial intelligence is like a kaleidoscope of colors — every time you look at it, you'll find something new.

Types of AI Systems

From AI's two sub-components, symbolic learning and machine learning, we can break each component down further into various other branches. The focus of this book lies with machine learning and its components, rather than symbolic learning. But it is necessary to understand both parts that form AI so that you can have a clear overview of what AI is. Below, I provide an explanation of how each component of AI breaks into various other divisions.

Symbolic Learning

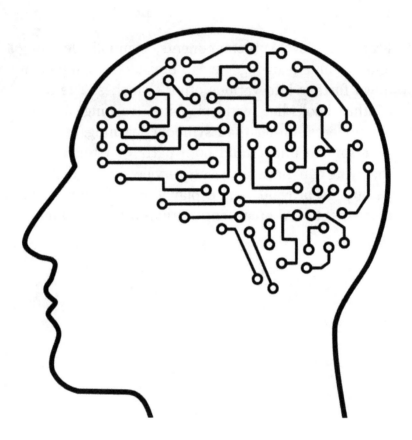

Symbolic learning is a method of imitating how humans learn. Humans learn through recognizing objects or people and understanding the relationship between those objects (and the person or other objects). Symbolic learning replicates this process by using rules to understand how objects work together.

For symbolic learning to work, it needs to have a database of all the symbols and possible relations — which, as you can imagine, is almost impossible. So, to prevent a person from having to manually capture a gazillion objects and relations, programs that learn symbolically are programmed to learn through a process called inference.

The inference is done by providing the program with a database that includes symbols and relations, and when it encounters new information, it can make a logical inference on where the additional information should be filed. For example, if we describe a sandwich as something with meat between bread, then a hotdog would be classified as a sandwich as well (CrashCourse, 2019, 03:15-05:21). But this brings up a conundrum because a hotdog isn't a sandwich, so the rule given has to be specific and encompass as many truths as possible. To create these differentiations involves a lot of mathematics which would take another book to explain!

Following the example, you can see that one of the biggest issues that are presented when dealing with symbolic learning is that the rules can be difficult to define so that a computer understands them. Computers are logical and currently cannot process the nuances that humans can. Although rules can be changed when dealing with symbolic AI, there is a "difficulty revising beliefs once encoded in a rules engine" (Nicholson, n.d.) so, if there is a change in how a symbol is perceived, it would be difficult to change that perception within the program because changing the rule doesn't remove what was 'learned'. Think of it as the human equivalent of 'old dogs can't learn new tricks.' We can further divide symbolic learning into two fields: that of robotics and computer vision.

Robotics is a subdiscipline of both AI and engineering. Robotics combines these two disciplines to create intelligent machines. The mobile element is from engineering while the intelligence is from AI. Robots can also be equipped with a combination of symbolic learning and machine learning.

Computer vision is the study and attempts to get computers to 'perceive' and interpret the world the same way humans do through visuals. For example: if you look at a red-hot stove plate, you would instinctively know not to touch it because you would know that it is hot. However, if you saw a red dinner plate on the stove, you would be cautious about touching it (it could be hot) but you wouldn't shy away from it. These reactions are from the visual stimuli that you get. For a computer to do this, you would need a precise description of what constitutes dangerous. To explain in simpler terms — when programming a computer to react to stimuli or categorize them, you would need to explain that the color alone is not what makes the situation dangerous. If the computer simply thought that the color of something made it dangerous — it would rank a red-colored dinner plate as a threat or danger.

For symbolic learning to take place, a lot of image processing needs to occur. The image processing also falls under machine learning so it will be explained more in-depth when we deal with machine learning in chapter 2. For the purpose of understanding, I will briefly explain what machine learning is.

Machine Learning

Machine learning is another branch of AI and it can be best explained as a machine that is programmed to learn. Thus, unlike symbolic learning, where the program 'learns' through classification that is based on the rule given, a machine learning system learns through data interpretation. These interpretations are gained through the use of algorithms.

We can break machine learning into two further divisions: statistical learning and deep learning.

Statistical learning encompasses speech recognition and natural language processing (NLP). Deep learning includes the creation of neural networks, which cause learning as we understand it to actually occur.

Machine learning and symbolic learning are the two components that make up AI. Now that you have an understanding of what these components are, let's look at the history of AI so you can understand just how far we've progressed.

History of AI

Allow me to take you on a winding tour through the peaks and valleys that characterize AI by furnishing you with the history of it. Although there is no clear indication of when the concept of AI was invented, we can determine that it became a field within the scientific community in the 1950s. Before that, there were numerous mentions or indications of it in a variety of science-fiction works.

In the 1700s and 1800s, authors like Jonathan Swift and Samuel Butler referred to machines that could possess a form of intelligence (Gulliver's Travels' 'The engine') or artificial consciousness (Erewhon). By the early 1900s, the concept of intelligent machines, called robots, began a huge trend in the sci-fi world of books and films. Some artists had these intelligent machines wreak havoc and destruction, which can be seen in the 1927 film called 'Metropolis'. While other artists had themes of rebellion where robots would stage a coup and take over the human race, which can be seen in the 1920 play *Czech Rossumovi Univerzalni Roboti.*

1943: Scientists nurture the concept of AI.

Although the world was being ravaged by the second world war, there is one great breakthrough that this period gave us: a reason for great minds to gather, albeit for sometimes sinister reasons.

In the context of AI, one of the minds we have to thank for setting the bar for AI is that of Alan Turing. Alan Turing was an English mathematician that contributed greatly to computer science (Wikipedia contributors, 2021c), and his Turing Test asks the question: *What if a machine could fool a person into thinking that it was a person?* This question set the bar for what would later be considered AI or simply a machine that could process commands.

1955: The term AI is coined.

Although the concept of a machine being intelligent was around for years, it was many years after the Turing Test was created that the term 'Artificial

Intelligence' got coined. It was coined by a group of researchers who submitted a proposal for a "research project on artificial intelligence" (McCarthy et al., 1955). Their proposal subsequently provided a framework upon which the academic discipline was built.

Unfortunately, the outcome of the research project did not yield the expected results for a variety of reasons. However, according to John McCarthy, one of the researchers, the research project failed partly due to insufficient funding, as well as the researchers having their own agendas (McCarthy, 2006). If you've ever worked on a group project, you can empathize with McCarthy because a lack of focus is detrimental to any group endeavor. Even though the workshop was not a raging success, it ensured that AI became an official branch within the scientific community.

1956-1961: Diving into the research of AI and the first robotic arm created.

Before funding can be given to creating prototypes, research has to be done and sponsors to carry out and aid in the implementation of the proposed research need to be found. As such, it was a while before anything tangible was created in the field of AI. Between 1955 and 1961, a lot of research was done that would later become the foundation for artificial intelligence systems.

In 1958, Frank Rosenblatt developed the Perceptron: it is an algorithm that is used for classification purposes (Wikipedia contributors, 2021d). This algorithm provided a base for supervised learning, a type of machine learning.

In the same year, researcher John McCarthy created LISP, a programming language that is later used for almost all AI research, thus overtaking Fortran, the language created the previous year. LISP essentially allowed data and the code to be represented in lists, which made it easy to manipulate and the language was flexible enough that it could be expanded upon (Jones, 2017) which made it great to use.

In 1959 computer scientist Arthur Samuel coined the term 'machine learning' (Gil Press, 2016) after ascertaining that a machine can be programmed to learn how to play checkers better than the person who programmed the machine. During this time, being able to play strategy games like checkers and chess was the mark of intelligence.

Unfortunately, scientists did not have the resources or capabilities to create AI programs or powered robots that would show that their theories were plausible. But the research and assumptions did not go to waste because their theories provided rich fodder for later scientists, once the capabilities and resources were made available.

In 1961 there was finally something tangible that the average person could grapple with in terms of AI. The first industrial robot was created — this robot could work much faster than humans and there was less of a risk to the humans. Unimate was invented by George Devol in the 1950s, but it was only produced in 1961 after having been worked on for almost 10 years. Unimate was not a robot as you and I currently know them. Rather, it was a robotic arm that could weld parts to car bodies faster than a human.

By incorporating Unimate, General Motors was able to automate their factory and lead in factory automation. After its success at General Motors, it was enlisted by other automobile manufacturers such as BMW, Volvo, and Mercedes Benz (Robotic Industries Association, n.d.).

1964: Advances in Natural Language Processing (NPL)

Daniel Bobrow developed a computer program called STUDENT using McCarthy's LISP programming language. The program understood natural language, a feat at the time. Natural language understanding is when a computer can understand the languages of humans (Expert.ai, 2021). The program solved algebra word problems.

In the same year, Joseph Weizenbaum created a program called ELIZA which in today's terms would be called a 'chatbot'. ELIZA uses Natural Language Processing (NPL) and was one of the first test subjects for Turing's test due to its capability to maintain a conversation. ELIZA was created to display the superficiality of thinking that a machine could be intelligent based solely on the ability to hold a conversation.

ELIZA was unable to pass the Turing test because she could not hold a proper conversation. Rather, it simply responded to the prompts within your sentences. After having a prolonged discussion with ELIZA, you would come to realize that she could only respond at a superficial level. There was no depth to her conversational abilities. Simply put, ELIZA could respond only to prompts and could not learn how to hold a conversation in the same way that a child would be able to learn. If you are interested in seeing how ELIZA holds a conversation then you can chat to a version of ELIZA by going onto the New Jersey Institute of Technology's website and searching for 'ELIZA.'

1965: Advancements in Expert systems

Scientists at Stanford started working on an 'expert system.' Expert systems are computer programs that mimic the decision-making of a human expert (Moné, 2020). The system is called DENDRAL and was written in LISP; it aimed to shorten the time that it took organic chemists to make decisions and solve problems. Expert systems like this are usually found within machine learning.

1966: Advancements in robotics

Once scientists were able to create a robotic arm, a chatbot, and a program that could mimic decision-making processes, they then created what was described as the first "the first electronic person," (New Atlas, 2015). This 'person' was a combination of robotics, vision, and spatial awareness.

The robot was named Shakey and was considered revolutionary because it was the first robot at the time that could move, identify obstacles, and avoid them! Shakey could also group boxes according to instructions and locate specific areas within "a 7-room environment" (SRI International, 2020). Shakey was not only an advancement in robotics but also a giant leap for the field of AI. The success of Shakey meant that computer scientists were able to later develop systems that provided GPS coordinates at the touch of a button, and it also provided the base technology that was used for the Mars Rovers that NASA sent into space (SRI International, 2020).

1968: Artistic interpretation and AI excitement

By this time, there is a lot of wonder at the ability of AI and how it can contribute to the world. However, humans are easily scared. In 1968, the fictitious movie 2001: A Space Odyssey was released. The movie is set in a spacecraft called 'Discovery One' which is en route to another planet. In the film, one of the main antagonists is an AI computer named HAL (short for Heuristically programmed ALgorithm). Initially, HAL seems to be a protagonist and is of great help to the astronauts. Unfortunately, HAL then malfunctions, seemingly without reason. The humans on the ship attempt to disconnect HAL, but the computer thwarts their plans, showing a sort of twisted survival instinct. HAL kills many of the astronauts on board to survive. The movie ends 'happily' because the malfunctioning AI robot is shut down and the main character survives. There is a second movie that explains why HAL malfunctioned, but the seed of fear of AI taking over was already planted. The fact that the AI system was relied upon so heavily, and then 'turned', is perhaps part of the reason that the AI winter occurred 6 years later.

Computer scientist Terry Winograd developed a program named SHRDLU which provides another block in the foundation for natural language processing. In essence, a person using the program could instruct SHRDLU to move the objects around on the screen, and the program could respond by moving the blocks or answering questions about your statements about the blocks, thus showing a sense of understanding (Wikipedia contributors, 2020).

The success of the program amazed many and raised everyone's expectations about the growth and viability of AI. However, the excitement was short-lived because SHRDLU could not function in other settings (Armstrong, 2014) which effectively nullified its intelligence. The program SHRDLU was confined to its block world in terms of its understanding and could not adapt to any other context.

1969: Backpropagation Theory — A mathematical way to get better predictions.

Backpropagation is a mathematical expression that allows computers to calculate the difference between the prediction and the actual solution through backtracking (Sood, 2019). In the simplest terms, backpropagation is learning through trial and error. While the theory was not of much use in 1969, it was an exceptional theory to be used in later AI systems.

1972: Resistance against AI

In July 1972, Professor Sir James Lighthill, a Professor of Applied Mathematics at Cambridge University, wrote a scathing report in which he stated that tasks like face recognition would be beyond AI's reach (Lighthill, 1972). However, as we currently know, AI has advanced incredibly, and its capabilities far surpass what he thought it would not be able to do.

1974-1980: AI Winter: The defunding of AI

Until now, AI was popular and being funded on the basis that it would yield better results. Unfortunately, there simply wasn't enough computing power or resources to create AI systems and innovations any faster than they were already being made.

1974 marked the dawn of the AI winter. Much like a cold war that is silently being waged, the AI winter silenced the AI community. The blanket of silence brought with it a lack of funding because of the antagonistic attitude that was garnered. There isn't just one reason for the AI winter, but it was rather an accumulation of reasons. In terms of artistic portrayal, intelligent robots and computers were shown as mutinous and evil for the most part. This did not ease society's mind, especially after the distinguished Professor Sir Lighthill made his proclamation and caused the loss of government support for the advancement of artificial intelligence. (Gil Press, 2016). Slowly but surely, more AI specialists lost their funding and AI became a deserted field.

1997: AI Research re-surges.

But, the genius of AI refused to be silenced for long. The AI winter eventually ended in the 1990s and funding started pouring in for research. In 1997, an AI system called Deep Blue was created, a program that could play chess. At the time, people who were able to play chess were recognized as highly intelligent, more so than someone who could play checkers. Deep Blue was built by IBM and beat Garry Kasparov, a then reigning champion at chess, thus reigniting the excitement about the possibilities of AI.

Although it may currently seem like this isn't a feat — in terms of the technology and information available at the time, this was incredible. Deep Blue focused on the intellectual faculties — at the time, chess was one of the epitomes of intelligence. Unfortunately, chess has a finite amount of moves that can be made which means that instead of a thinking AI, Deep Blue was reactive.

1998: The mark of an intelligent being.

One of the things that AI forced many to consider was what constituted intelligence? Deep Blue focused on intellectual capabilities, so it made sense for the next facet that scientists attempted to 'clone' to be emotional abilities. Scientists attempted to recreate the emotional faculties of a person by creating a robot named Kismet. Kismet was able to demonstrate some social and emotional features, such as getting 'uncomfortable' when you got too close and showing a range of emotions such as surprise, anger, and happiness.

1999: Man's best friend recreated.

In 1999, a robot dog called AIBO was created by Sony, which could develop a personality over time, walk as well as 'see' where it was going and understand spoken commands (Wikipedia contributors, 2021a). This was a step toward integrating AI into daily life.

2002: AI in the home

By the 2000s, AI was no longer a stranger to the public. AIBO was a huge success with children. The next step was to integrate an AI machine for adults. This is the main difference as to why AIBO and Roomba were created, the audience they pertained to. The integration of Roomba served as a precursor for the acceptance of AI in daily life. Roomba is an amazing little AI-powered vacuum that can learn your schedule, clean easily, and even empty itself. This brought AI into homes and slowly started carving out a new normal.

2011: Virtual Assistants and Human compatible robots

By 2011, enough of the world was using 'smart' technology that a virtual assistant was created. Siri was the world's first virtual assistant that could remind you of events and schedule them, just to name a few of her capabilities. The success of Siri provided space for other tech moguls like Google to create the assistants that we know now. These assistants are constantly being updated so that they use Big Data to keep them updated and improved.

In addition to Siri, the world also saw its first robot that was able to answer questions posed in simple everyday language. The credit for this invention is given to IBM, who created the robot and named it Watson. Watson's ability to understand human language and respond as opposed to commands demonstrated natural language processing in a robot. Previous robots could answer specific questions in much the same way that ELIZA could, but Watson was different.

Watson was able to answer questions in the same way that a human would be able to. He was so successful that he even won the quiz show called Jeopardy.

Unfortunately, Watson was unable to pass the Turing test because he could not demonstrate the intellectual capacity to have an in-depth conversation. Rather, Watson was able to answer questions that were factual and could be extracted from its large databases.

2014: Alexa says hello.

Created by Amazon, Alexa is another personal assistant which took the market by storm — but instead of having just an assistant on your phone, Alexa was embedded in a range of products that effectively created a 'SMART' home where you can control your home through electronics. This was new and exciting and offered a new way for people to live. With Alexa, you would not need to get out of bed to turn the lights off — you could simply ask Alexa to switch the lights off for you.

2016: Humanoids.

2016 saw two humanoid bots that were created in two different spheres. A humanoid bot is a robot that is created to look like a human or interact like one.

Tay was a chatbot that was released by Microsoft and allowed to converse with thousands of people on Twitter to learn through conversation. However, in less than a day, Tay had learned the worst of humanity's traits such as transphobia and racism (Vincent, 2016).

Sophia, the other humanoid bot, was created in the hopes of producing a framework for "understanding human-robot interactions and their potential service and entertainment applications" (Hanson Robotics Limited, 2020). Sophia is also the first robot to have citizenship — she is a registered citizen of Saudi Arabia.

2017: AlphaGo

By 2017, AI and robots seemed to be the new best thing in homes. There was a lot of talk about Sophia the robot and the possibilities that she represented. In 2017, a company called OpenAI made major strides with a project called AlphaGO.

Without diving into the mathematics of it — AlphaGo was the first robot that was able to win the game Go. Unlike chess which has a finite number of moves, Go has an infinite number of possible ways to win. Chess can be won based on weighing the statistics of your opponent playing a certain move based on their prior moves. Go, on the other hand, is not as straightforward and requires more strategic thinking.

2018: Ethical issues in AI

One of the biggest advancements in AI in 2018 was the OpenAI Five team, which was a team of five neural networks that played a game of DOTA2. Although the bots lost, they were able to compete and that in itself is amazing because DOTA2 requires the type of teamwork that only humans have been able to display.

Although there weren't many huge advancements in AI products or uses in 2018, numerous ethical issues arose.

Google's I/O conference in May 2018 revealed an additional feature added to the Google Assistant called Duplex, which could make calls on behalf of the user to book appointments (Dickson, 2018). While AI assistants were, and are hugely popular, many worried that with this added feature, these assistants could be used for unsavory purposes that aren't too sweet either. Issues such as impersonating others or being used in scams because these assistants sounded human were some of the raised issues. To combat this, Google added in more security changes: it immediately identifies itself as a Google Assistant and tells the person receiving the call that the call is being recorded.

Another ethical issue that has been raised is to do with facial recognition that has been improved significantly by advances in deep learning but is quite reminiscent of big brother. Additionally, providing facial recognition technology for the public could provide more access than necessary for ill-intended people, such as stalkers. Additionally, facial technology is not entirely accurate, which has also led to a lot of controversies. The president of Microsoft, Brad Smith, has penned a powerful post that addresses the concerns relating to facial recognition in government spheres, stating that the government must be proactive about managing how the technology is used so that it does not cause problems.

These are just two of the ethical issues that have been noted in 2018, and we have come to the conclusion that AI must be augmented rather than simply left to 'learn' by itself. The reason for this is that AI algorithms, while awesome, will also 'inherit and amplify our individual and societal biases' (Dickson, 2018).

2019: New advancements

In 2019, there were a few breakthroughs that are notable (and may influence the public directly). These include:

OpenAI's robot hand was able to solve a physical Rubik's cube thereby demonstrating 'intelligence' and dexterity that is new for robots.

Deepfake is arguably one of the scarier AI systems that became popular. Deepfake's system can take a single photo and create a video. This raised concerns because the application made it easier to create and spread fake news.

Upside down reinforcement learning is created. Essentially, this means that a supervised system can learn new skills through imitation rather than focusing on rewards in the traditional behavioral sense. This is great because machine learning systems will need less time to be trained (Yadav, 2020).

2020—2021: Technology becomes a necessity.

The pandemic that COVID-19 brought put a lot of strain on online platforms, which means that incorporating AI systems were of paramount importance. The changes that were brought about in 2020 will continue to shape 2021.

- AI systems were used to develop the COVID-19 vaccine. AI systems were able to sort through all the information and also provide predictions on mutations. Baidu is a Chinese company that specializes in AI and it paired its AI systems called LinearFold and LinearDesign with the National Institute for Viral Disease Control and Prevention (Baidu, 2021) to integrate AI systems in the process of creating other vaccines. Using AI systems will enable healthcare to respond quicker to another outbreak.
- Quantum computing is being researched and has the potential to revolutionize AI systems because quantum computing means we will have even more computing power. More computing power means that we can process Big Data even better and that can provide better input for AI systems.

The field of AI is expected to grow much larger, especially in light of us being in the fourth industrial revolution.

Benefits of AI being used?

There are many benefits of AI being used; both for businesses and the average person. Automation of jobs, with the addition of AI, is one of the biggest benefits for both businesses and the public because it provides so much scope for opportunity.

Businesses

By including AI in businesses, there will be the following benefits:

- Businesses will be more likely to expand quickly and will need about half of the human capital with the integration of various AI systems (Raj Ramesh, 2017b, 03:15-05:21).

From a monetary standpoint, this is great for the business because they will have less expenditure. However, from the perspective of the job market, most people think that the incorporation of AI will mean that the job market will be made narrower. But, research from the World Economic Forum (WEF) shows that as many jobs are being eliminated, more will be created. Fortunately, contrary to popular misconception, AI will not be able to just 'run' businesses on their own. To function correctly and efficiently, AI systems need to work in tandem with their human counterparts; thus, the nature of human jobs will change as the workforce landscape changes.

- When coupled with Big Data, AI will be able to help companies be more attuned to their customer base so they can serve them efficiently. Unlike humans, AI can analyze and see patterns in vast amounts of data. Those patterns will be helpful because they will inform the choices businesses make. In keeping up with the customer's demands, the company is able to transform their products and services as well as upskill their employees.

The average person

To become eligible in the new AI workforce you will need to upskill yourself to the extent that an AI system will be unable to do your job. While AI seems excellent and able to do so much more than a human can do — it has a few flaws: AI systems cannot integrate and understand information and data as well as humans, and they are currently unable to be creative. Thus, AI is beneficial because it will allow humans to capitalize on their own uniqueness. For AI to function, there has to be some sort of logical and rational relational rule to guide the AI.

- Many services will be bettered with the use of AI. For example, delivery services will be improved if AI is used to predict routes because it will choose the shortest routes.

- Health care can be made more universal. With everyone having a smartphone, having an AI system that can provide a pre-diagnosis of a person based on symptoms can greatly reduce the amount of time spent in queues. Imagine going to a hospital and instead of having to fill out all the forms before being admitted for consultation, the doctor will already have an idea of what you could have based on the symptoms that you present. Naturally, the AI system will not be the doctor — but a raised scaly red and circular rash that itches is likely to be ringworm.

- AI can help you with your financial issues. No longer will you have to struggle with filing your taxes nor will you have to worry about your taxes being embezzled. The integration of AI systems in the financial sectors will make your experience better because the filing of taxes can be automated (Joshi, 2020).
- Learning and teaching will become easier with AI because it will be able to analyze the behaviors and marks of students, thereby alerting you about students that need your attention.
- Your online presence will be greatly personalized. Many online businesses have already integrated AI systems into their business models (Joshi, 2020). Companies like Spotify, Amazon, and Netflix use AI to see how their customers interact with their content; that information is then analyzed, and new marketing strategies are employed to make the products appeal to the customer again. Furthermore, these algorithms allow you to find more things that are similar to the things that you enjoy.
- Risky jobs like plumbing can be overtaken by AI robots, therefore, limiting the plumber's risk of contracting a disease. Jobs that pose a risk due to their position, rather than the nature of the job, will also be overtaken by AI. For example, bank tellers will no longer be at risk

of being held hostage by robbers because AI will be able to take over the duties of the teller efficiently.

- Services that include manual data capturing will be improved. This means that services like the creation of identity documents or leases will have fewer errors.
- There will be more jobs when AI is used — although it seems counterintuitive because AI will allow businesses to use less manpower to work — it will encourage an evolution of the job market. (Editors, Forbes Technology Council, 2018). The reason for this evolution is that AI will provide aid to humans so they will be able to perform better. Think of AI as being like a calculator that you can use to check if you correctly calculated something. Although the downside is that some reliance will be created — provided that humans don't lose the skills and knowledge of how to do what the AI is doing, then the introduction of AI into the general world of the public will be great.
- The introduction and implementation of AI will allow automation to be done with more speed and efficiency. Although there is currently some fear that AI will take over the world and cause a loss of control, these fears are unwarranted in the same way that fears of the second industrial revolution were unwarranted. Electricity has not taken over our lives and has created dozens of new ways for us

to work and make our lives easier. Unfortunately, the creation of electricity has warranted some environmental concerns, but these are being researched so that these concerns can be addressed. As such, the concerns raised about AI will also be addressed.

- AI will render jobs that are repetitive and 'mundane' as obsolete as new programs can do it quicker and more efficiently. While this takes some jobs off of the market — it also introduces a wide arena of other jobs that AI cannot do but are uniquely human. These jobs are those that are creative and innovative in nature.

The integration and use of artificial intelligence in daily life have many benefits and as the technology progresses, it will become even more beneficial.

What's the future of AI?

"I believe [AI] is going to change the world more than anything in the history of mankind. More than electricity." — Kai Fu Lee

With the extraordinary advancements that AI has made, and is continuing to make, the possibilities are endless when there are so many avenues to consider when wondering what the future of AI is to be.

Currently, great strides are being made in AI — these advances are so great that we are currently entering the 4th Industrial Revolution. The 4th Industrial Revolution has become something of a buzzword. To explain briefly, it is the continued "automation of manufacturing and industrial practices" that will be using technology that is powered by AI.

If you would like to learn more about AI and, perhaps, even pursue studies in it, then there are a few different ways that you can do this. The path you take to learn skills that are relevant to joining the force that is improving and creating AI will largely be dependent on your financial and temporal capacity.

Short courses:

You can take a variety of short courses on AI through online course providers such as Udemy or Coursera. These courses can be as broad or narrow as you'd like to learn. Both institutes also have frequent sales so you can do these short courses without spending an arm and a kidney if you wait for their discounted rates.

Most universities and colleges also provide short online courses, but you will have to contact the institute to find out more on how to apply for their short courses. A great example of a short online course on AI includes the one offered by Oxford University in the United Kingdom. The course is 6 weeks long and will provide you with an overview of AI, as well as the various applications thereof.

Naturally, the courses that you take will be determined by what your ultimate goal is. A person who is interested in knowing about current trends will take a course that is centered more on understanding what AI is and how it affects the world, while a person that plans on carving a career in AI will look at courses that are more technical.

Careers/Jobs:

At a university or college level, you can sign up for computer science degrees and then specialize in any one of the various components of AI. AI is broad so there are a myriad of careers that you can get into if you decide to specialize in AI after completing your computer science degree. The list provided here is by no means exhaustive and it will cover jobs that are not related to Big Data or machine learning. Jobs for machine learning and Big Data are discussed in chapters 2 and 3, respectively.

Robotics and AI scientist

A robotics scientist has to be able to build and maintain robots. While not all robots are powered by AI, the Robotics and AI scientist needs to be able to engineer the robot and use the applicable AI system within it so that it can do the job needed. To get into this degree, you would typically need to complete an engineering degree and then also have some form of AI programming qualification.

Computer Vision Engineer

Computer Vision Engineers work with data and apply the necessary algorithms to the data. The data that Computer Vision Engineers work with is typically those of a visual nature. This data can then be processed and meaning can be derived from it so it can be used. Computer Vision engineers are those that will help when creating robots such as Shaky who are able to navigate areas based on visual stimuli.

NLP Engineers

Natural Language Processing engineers create devices that can understand human languages so that they can analyze and generate a response or complete an action. In addition to this, NLP engineers should also have some basic data science and machine learning skills so that they can teach the programs how to understand the finer facets of language (Ray, 2021). You can see the work of NLP engineers when you use translation applications.

In summary

Artificial Intelligence is a broad field of study that has a rich history even though it is a youthful 71 years old. Much like all fields of study, it goes through its own troughs and peaks. Through viewing the history, we were able to understand the ups and downs that the discipline went through, as well as get insight into some of the misconceptions that people had.

Currently, we are seeing a huge resurgence in AI and it is, without a doubt, deeply ingrained in our lives in the same way that electricity was. While there are some concerns that we may become too dependent on AI, experts have suggested that AI cannot function without human input, so it will be years before AI becomes 'sentient' in the way that is displayed in 2001: Space Odyssey. Examples of AI that's used in our everyday life that you might not have thought of include Google Translate. This application has improved significantly and provides a simple method for people to communicate across languages. While it's still in its infancy, I have no doubt that it will improve as more people use it.

"A baby learns to crawl, walk and then run. We are in the crawling stage when it comes to applying machine learning." — Dave Waters

Chapter 2: Machine Learning

MACHINE
LEARNING

Machine learning is a branch of AI that further breaks into Statistical learning and Deep learning. Machine learning works through the recognition of patterns. These patterns allow the machine to learn from its errors without being programmed to (IBM Cloud Education, 2020). Machine learning is being used in a wide variety of industries for its ability to make jobs easier through automation or augmentation.

When we speak about automation through machine learning, we refer to machines that are able to do the same job that a person could with such efficiency that the human can be replaced. Jobs that are automated are typically those that are monotonous. Augmentation means that machines are able to supplement the work that a person is doing rather than take over completely. An example of this includes software that aids analysts in deriving insights from data.

Categories of Machine Learning

There are two broad categories within machine learning: statistical learning and deep learning. These two further break into speech recognition, natural language processing, convoluted neural networks, and recursive neural networks. Each of these categories within machine learning looks at different elements of human intelligence. Remember, machine learning is a component of AI, and it seeks to mimic human intelligence with the aim of improving upon it.

Statistical Learning

Statistical learning is the umbrella term for learning through understanding and prediction by using statistics based on data. Statistical learning breaks into speech recognition and natural language processing.

Speech recognition is the capability of a program to 'process human speech into a written format' (IBM Cloud Education, 2020a). Speech recognition that uses deep learning will be able to learn more efficiently the more it interacts with language. AI can also ensure that speech recognition is trained to identify different people talking, omit vulgarity, learn jargon or exclude noises from the business. Examples, where this is shown, are on the video conferencing platform called Google Meet, which allows you to enable the voice-to-text function. When enabled, the algorithm automatically picks up that a different person is speaking, therefore preventing the speech of multiple people from being in one sentence. Applications like Discord use programs like Krisp that exclude noises other than the speaker's voice which prevents background noise from interfering with the conversation. The advances in speech recognition are great, especially now that Big Data can aid in the training of machine learning systems. Closed captions on YouTube have improved tenfold now that speech recognition has progressed. This progression means that those who need speech recognition because they are hard of hearing or seeing will be able to use the tools efficiently.

Natural Language processing is how computers understand human language in a way that can be used internally. A great way to understand natural language processing is to think of the way that your virtual assistant responds to you when you ask a question. Your virtual assistant can understand you even if you use natural fillers like 'um' or pause briefly between your instructions. Natural language processing allows for effective communication between machines and humans.

Deep Learning

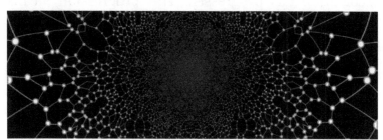

Deep learning is concerned with recognising the patterns in data and reacting, or learning, about it in the same way that humans do. Deep learning uses something called neural networks, which are fashioned after the structure of a human brain. There are two branches of deep learning: convoluted neural networks (CNN) and recursive neural networks (RNN). Unlike symbolic learning, deep learning takes place by using data that has more depth. Symbolic learning takes place primarily with symbols and images, which can be described as one dimension in mathematical terms, while deep learning takes place and can learn through multidimensional data which includes videos, images, and text.

Convoluted neural networks (CNN) are networks that process images. CNN's are the building blocks for image processing. They interpret images by analyzing them with a filter and then identifying the patterns or objects in the image. You can imagine this process by thinking of yourself taking graph paper and asking a few different people to write the letter 'A' on the page. Each person will write the letter differently, but after analyzing the letters, you will be able to note the patterns of how each person writes. However, as you can imagine, for a CNN to work, it must have the correct image or pattern to compare the variation to. Similarly to how you would need to know what the letter 'A' looks like, being able to recognize that someone wrote the letter A instead of H. AI systems that use CNN will initially produce random results, but after being fed more data it will become more accurate at deciphering the patterns. CNN is primarily used for image processing because it is unable to handle media such as videos and blocks of text (Ambalina, 2020).

Recursive neural networks (RNN) are networks that can process information that is in the sequence, which means that RNNs can process media such as videos and blocks of text. To do this processing, RNNs have a reference point outside of the data that it is being fed and can then predict what information you are feeding it. A great example of this is auto-correct. For this example, for simplicity, I will only be referring to the spelling of a word. A dictionary's worth of words is loaded into the database of the autocorrect RNN. When you type and give 'input' the system looks at the similarity of your word to the words it has within its database. Based on that, it will then give you a prediction of what the 'correct' spelling should be. Should you use a word that is not in its database, but you use the word often enough the neural network will add that to its database so that its predictions can be more accurate to your typing.

There are autocorrect systems that look at more dimensions before giving predictions — take a look at Grammarly that takes into account the syntax, grammar, and spelling of your sentences to give you suggestions. Much like with every other component of AI, it is not infallible and can sometimes provide 'incorrect' recommendations.

Types of ML Algorithms

There are three main ways that machine learning takes place. Machine learning can be supervised, unsupervised, or through reinforcement.

Supervised learning is when learning in machine learning is when a machine has to be trained before it can start learning. This training includes feeding the system with data that is already labelled. For example, if you wanted to know the shortest way to get to your friend's house — you would first need to know the various ways to get there before you would be able to determine which would be the shortest route. Similarly, before supervised learning can take place, it needs to have data that is already labelled and categorized before it will be able to deal with new data. This type of learning is great for classifying new data based on characteristics (or patterns).

- *The nearest neighbor*

  The nearest neighbor algorithm is a supervised learning algorithm because it needs to have a database before it can begin to classify any new information. Thus, a human needs to feed the algorithm with information so that it can differentiate between existing information.

The nearest neighbor algorithm classifies new information by looking at which set of information it is closest to. Imagine that you have two datasets — one cluster shows the information on the size of jalapeno peppers while the other cluster shows the size of ghost peppers. Once your machine can differentiate between the ghost peppers and jalapeno peppers, you then add another pepper that is unlabeled, and this pepper falls somewhere in between. The nearest neighbor will then calculate the distance between the new unlabeled pepper and the other two clusters of peppers to determine which one the new pepper should be part of. If the unlabeled pepper is closer to the jalapeno peppers than the ghost peppers, then it will be clustered underneath the jalapeno peppers.

An example of the nearest neighbor algorithm being used is when a company analyzes their data and recommends things that you would like. For example, continuing on our earlier peppers example — if we were looking at what types of peppers people bought and wanted to sell a new pepper, we would be able to determine that people who enjoyed the ghost peppers would enjoy the new pepper because it is similar. Many companies that have 'recommended for you' tabs on their page use a variant of the nearest neighbor algorithm.

- *Random Forest*

  The random forest algorithm is another simple yet important algorithm in machine learning. The random forest is fed with information based on certain parameters which are then grouped and when new information is added, it places it into one of the clusters and generates the average pattern.

To illustrate, Alicia wants to choose a career, but she's not sure what to choose. She then asks her teacher, who asks what she's interested in and what she has no interest in at all. These questions set a sort of boundary for the response that the teacher gives. Alicia does not like mathematics so the teacher will not tell Alicia to study something that has foundations in mathematics like statistics or Big Data.

After speaking to her teacher, Alicia has an idea of various careers, but she decides to speak to more people. As she speaks to more people, they give responses to her question in relation to the boundaries that she has given. In the end, Alicia looks at all the data and decides on the career that has been recommended most to her. This is how the random forest algorithm works.

The random forest algorithm can be seen at work in the financial sector where it is used to determine which client is more likely to repay their loans or predict a stock's future behavior (Dickson, 2018).

- *Decision Tree*

The decision tree algorithm is similar to the random forest, but instead of combining "several different decisions, the decision tree only combines a few" (Vadapalli, 2020), which means that the decision tree algorithm is a better choice if you want to get faster results. But, due to the lesser information in a decision tree, it is less stable than a random forest (Singhal, 2020).

Decision trees classify information by sorting through them and checking whether they match certain characteristics. If the characteristic is not matched, then the outcome differs from when it is matched.

A great example of decision trees are the quizzes that used to appear in magazines to find out your personality test. You would need to answer the first question with one of the answers provided. Once you answered that, you would continue answering questions and each answer would take you in one of two directions. For instance: Do you like apples? If yes, the next question would be: do you prefer fruit over candy? if no, the next question would be do you prefer chocolate over jelly babies. And once you've answered enough questions, you would get down to the results which would tell you that you are either a health-conscious person who enjoys sweets or a person who needs to be more health-conscious.

Unsupervised learning is when learning takes place without any labelled data being fed to the system. This means that the data is put into the system and the system has to recognize the patterns by itself. Using an unsupervised learning algorithm means that human labor.

Unsupervised learning is similar to the way that a human learns. It isn't the same but similar. Imagine that every time you are put into a new situation at work, you get a migraine. Over time, you will learn to associate a new situation with the sudden onset of a migraine. No one told you that you will experience this migraine in a new situation, so you had to come to the conclusion yourself while thinking about other factors such as the seasons or if you were in contact with a sick person? After experiencing the situation enough times, you will find the correlation between new situations and your sudden migraine.

Similarly, unsupervised learning algorithms will also go through the same motions of processing data and 'incorrect' predictions until they find the correct correlation. While this example is quite simple, I hope it provides you with a visual of how unsupervised learning occurs.

- *Apriori Algorithm*

The apriori algorithm is one that creates groups of items based on the data it is fed. This algorithm improves the more data it is fed, and it gets its name from the fact that it uses 'prior knowledge' of things that are frequently grouped together. The apriori algorithm needs a large dataset to work with, so it will be inefficient and inaccurate if used with a small dataset.

For the apriori algorithm to work, it looks at three things within the dataset that it has. These three things are: support, confidence, and lift.

Support is to do with the consistency and velocity of the item. If we were using a supermarket as an example, the support would be how popular the new banana loaves of bread are. The popularity would be determined by the consistency and speed at which it is sold. You could calculate this by saying that:

> *Support = (Overall sales of banana bread) / (total sales)*
>
> > *= which will give you an idea of how popular the banana bread is.*

Confidence is how often the set of items are bought. For instance, if customers are buying both milk and banana bread then you need to look at the sales that involve both banana bread and milk. So, your equation will look something like this.

Confidence = (sales of banana bread AND milk)/ (total sales of banana bread)

= give you the idea of how many people buy both when shopping.

Lift is the increase you will see if you sell both items. The equation used is:

Lift = (confidence) / (support)

= likelihood of you selling both items instead of one.

The apriori algorithm is a favorite in retail stores because it informs them of the ways that they can boost sales by appealing to their customer's needs and behaviors.

- *Principal component analysis*

This method is best suited to data where you want to derive patterns that one is not aware of. The principal component analysis makes sure that the important data in the unlabelled dataset is pushed forward for analysis.

The principal component analysis is used often in industries like neuroscience where it can be used to determine if a neuron has action potential, which is what enables neurons to communicate with each other (Wikipedia contributors, 2021i).

Reinforcement learning is much closer to the actual way that humans learn than unsupervised learning. While unsupervised learning deals with the correlation between data that it receives, reinforcement learning uses an algorithm that uses a basis similar to the theory of behaviorism. The learning is trial-and-error with the premise that if the outcome is good, then it's 'rewarded' and if the outcome is bad, then it's 'punished.' Reinforcement learning requires a human to 'check' the results and provide reinforcement so that the machine can improve itself.

- *Q-Learning algorithm*

  This algorithm tells the system what action to take when faced with a certain decision and the behavior is reinforced through the reward. Therefore, if the reward is received based on the action, which is then repeated.

History of Machine Learning

Now that you have an overview of how machine learning takes place, let's take a look at all of the events that led to the use of machine learning that we see today. The history of machine learning is prolific.

1935: Alan Turing proposes a learning machine.

Alan Turing is credited with being the father of AI, but more specifically, he made amazing contributions to the machine learning subdiscipline of AI. In 1935, Turing proposed the concept of a machine that would be able to store information and then improve itself based on the stored information (Britannica, n.d.) which is seen as a foundation for deep learning.

1951: First neural network machine.

The first neural network machine was designed by cognitive and computer scientists Marvin Lee Minsky and Dean Edmonds. They called it SNARC, which is short for Stochastic Neural Analog Reinforcement Calculator. The machine was created using 'analog and electromechanical components' (Martinez, 2019), which included 40 artificial neurons depicted with lights that lit up to show how neural networks worked. The capacitors within the lights were able to store electrical energy long enough for it to have 'memory'.

This memory helped the algorithm learn the routes to take to get to the preset finish line.

1952: First machine playing checkers.

Computer scientist Arthur Samuel believed that teaching computers how to play games would be a great foundational start for computers to develop the ability to respond to real-world problems. In 1952, while working at IBM, he worked on what is known as one of the first neural network programs called the Samuel Checkers program. The program was able to learn by memorizing the moves that it encountered and played, thereby allowing it to calculate the reward probability of its movements. It was refined until the mid-70s when it could hold its own against an amateur player. It serves as one of the first examples of reinforcement learning.

The program was demonstrated on television on February 24, 1956. In 1962, the program played against a 'self-proclaimed checkers master' named Robert Nealey who, unfortunately (for him) lost to the computer. These events served to highlight the capabilities that computers using neural networks had.

1957: Perceptrons.

In 1957, American psychologist Frank Rosenblatt discovered perceptrons. According to Pearson Education, Frank Rosenblatt's discovery was the 'first algorithmically described neural network' (2018) and, as such, inspired the interest of other scientists to continue researching neural networks. Perceptrons, in a physical sense, can be described as the 'blocks' that build up neural networks. Perceptrons are usually used to classify data into two parts, which is why it is commonly used in supervised learning

1963: Machines play tic-tac-toe through learning.

In 1963, British AI researcher Donald Michie created the 'machine' Matchbox Educable Noughts And Crosses Engine (MENACE) that uses reinforcement learning to play a game called tic-tac-toe (or naughts and crosses). With the lack of computational power at the time, demonstrating how machine learning could take place by using mechanical means was a genius move. The 'machine' was actually 300 matchboxes with the stage of the game being played on it. Initially, when you start out with the game, the machine's moves are randomized but, as it loses, it 'learns' that those moves are not going to help it win and as it wins, it 'learns' how to continue winning.

1967: An algorithm called 'nearest neighbour' was created.

This algorithm was created and laid the foundation for pattern recognition. It is commonly used for classification purposes and also has a variant role in deciding which route delivery services should use.

1969: Limitations of perceptrons.

In 1969, Marvin Minksy, designer of the first neural network machine, co-published a book that provided some of the limitations of perceptrons and neural networks (Wikipedia contributors, 2020a). Unfortunately, the publication of Minsky's book 'Perceptrons' which detailed the limitations of neural networks and implied that the study should be halted, may have also been a contributing factor for the AI winter that came a few years later.

1985: NetTalk is created — a machine that learns words the same way a baby does.

In 1985, computer scientists Terrence Sejnowski and Charles Rosenberg created an artificial neural network that consisted of 300 neurons with the intention that it would 'explore the mechanisms of learning' (Wikipedia contributors, 2021a), which included how to pronounce English words from the text in much the same way a child would learn how to read.

Not only did this advancement help in the field of machine learning but it also provided some insight into how the human brain works (Times, 1988).

1992: TD backgammon uses Deep learning.

In 1992, a computer program was developed by Gerald Tesauro at IBM (Wikipedia contributors, 2020d) and while it functioned almost the same as every other reinforcement learning program — the key feature that made it stand out was the way it allowed 'behaviour' to be reinforced.

Once TD-Gammon played a game, it then updated weights in its neural net to reduce reaction time. The neural network in TD-Gammon functioned in almost the same way that muscle memory works.

1997: IBM Deep Blue beats chess master.

In 1997, the IBM computer called Deep Blue competed against a world chess champion and won. Not only was this an achievement for artificial intelligence as a discipline but it was also a leap for the subdiscipline of machine learning. The programming in Deep Blue allowed deep learning to be applied in other areas such as data mining, financial modelling, and molecular dynamics (IBM, n.d.).

2002: Deep Learning Library.

In 2002, a library consisting of deep learning algorithms was created and shared. Unfortunately, Torch is no longer in active development, but it is being substituted with a library called PyTorch (Wikipedia contributors, 2021c).

2006: The Netflix Prize.

With growing interest in machine learning and how it can improve business models, Netflix launched a competition titled 'Netflix Prize.' To win the competition, developers had to create an algorithm or improve Netflix for the 'prediction of user ratings for films' (Wikipedia contributors, 2021a). The competition lasted for 3 years before the team 'BellKor's Pragmatic Chaos' won the grand prize by improving Netflix's own algorithm by 10.09% accuracy (Wikipedia contributors, 2021a).

2009: ImageNet

ImageNet is similar to Torch in that it is a database for researchers. It provides an "easily accessible image database" (ImageNet, n.d.). What is remarkable about ImageNet is that there are over 14 million images that are all labelled so feeding your machine labelled data is simple, which, in turn, allows you to effectively train your machine.

2011—IBM Watson wins Jeopardy!

Watson won Jeopardy in 2011, which showcased its superior ability to understand and respond to questions asked in natural language. Watson's features included being able to process language, retrieve relevant information, and reason. Since 2011, the software running Watson has been upgraded and commercialized after its success.

2012: Google recognized cats!

The Google Brain team, which is a team that is tasked with researching deep learning AI at Google, was able to program a neural network to recognize cats even though it was fed unlabeled data.

2014: I know your face!

Facebook creates and publishes a neural network system that can identify faces with 97% accuracy. The success rate of this deep learning system even rivalled the human ability to recognize faces (Wikipedia contributors, 2020a). The identification of faces has been implemented and is constantly being improved upon. You use face recognition technology when you are tagging your friends on Facebook. If you use Google Photos, then you are aiding the neural network to identify faces because the system files photos according to the name of the person. For example, if you have many photos of Marie, then Google Photos will ask you to verify that some of these photos are indeed Marie. Where the photos are not Marie, the algorithm then learns how to discern between a Marie look alike and Marie.

2016: Machines learn to play GO!

Unlike chess, the game GO! has infinitely more winning combinations, so when the program AlphaZero was able to successfully beat a human at GO! by using machine learning, it highlighted just how far we have come from teaching a machine how to play and win a tic-tac-toe match.

2019: Machines learn to play DOTA2.

The computer game Defence of the Ancients (DOTA) requires a team effort to win — there are infinite ways to play the game because each character has its own modifications and abilities. There are 120 heroes in DOTA and each one has 4 abilities that can be upgraded multiple times. Additionally, there are abilities that you can earn based on milestones reached.

Between 2016 and 2019, OpenAI, an AI research and deployment company, created a bot that was able to beat a player when playing 1v1 (OpenAI, 2020). This was a huge leap in deep learning because the bot learned how to play DOTA2 through unsupervised learning and it does not use imitation or tree search, meaning that it doesn't mimic other players or search through vast repositories to make calculated decisions on how to play.

Examples of Machine Learning in different industries

Machine learning has infiltrated the world and is being used in various fields with great success. Below are the ways in which machine learning is used in different industries.

Security and surveillance services

Security services have integrated machine learning tools into their systems to detect and respond to threats, especially now that the pandemic of COVID-19 has changed the way we operate.

Health services

Image recognition has aided doctors in determining whether scans of patients' lungs are cancerous or not and chatbots that are able to use NPL are used to help doctors determine patterns in symptoms (Guerrouj, 2020).

Virtual Online World

There are many instances where machine learning is used in the virtual world:

- Voice searching and dialing on your smartphone is powered by machine learning.
- SMART appliances are usually also programmed using machine learning algorithms.
- Image recognition is used in an assortment of applications. One popular application that uses image recognition is Facebook. The tagging function allows the image to be processed and labelled.
- Digital platforms use machine learning algorithms to make their branding and marketing more efficient through tracking of 'user-generated content like reviews' (Roy, 2021).

- Chatbots are a common way that statistical learning is used in our daily lives.

Sales

The commercial sector is a huge space where machine learning has been implemented. You can easily see it in online stores like Takealot. Machine learning programs in retail are often geared to make the consumer want to purchase items and as such, after viewing certain items, the consumer will continuously get items that are similarly recommended.

Businesses are also using machine learning algorithms to ensure that their sales, marketing, and revenue are tracked so that they can be improved. Algorithms that analyze large amounts of data and plot it in easily interpreted images will help companies flourish.

Another element that is increasingly popular is sentiment analysis. Essentially, this is a machine learning algorithm that uses natural language processing to analyze whether a review is positive or negative. These reviews allow the business to take the necessary steps to ensure that the consumers are appeased by addressing negative feedback.

Traffic

Applications like Google Maps use machine learning algorithms to show you the correct routes when you look for directions. These algorithms sieve through data that includes where you've been, where you are, how you've previously reached the place if you've been there before, as well as searching the web for news of any issues relating to traffic. Traffic can be caused by a myriad of things such as national events or accidents — most of which will get reported using online platforms that the application's algorithm can access. Self-driving cars will also be using machine learning to function and wow, what a time it will be when self-driving cars are the new normal.

American taxi and delivery service company Uber uses machine learning to predict the estimated time for rides and meal delivery as well as to detect fraud (Richman, 2016).

Your Email

This may sound like an unlikely place for machine learning to be at work but it's an important feature in your email to prevent phishing and scamming. The spam filter on your email uses machine learning to identify and predict which messages are spam or are unsafe.

In addition to the spam filter, companies like Google have introduced something called 'Smart reply' which works like predictive text — except it predicts three words to complete your sentences.

Financial Services:

Many companies in the financial sector make use of machine learning to detect things like fraud and determine credit scores (Faggella, 2020). This is done through using neural networks and using machine learning algorithms to predict scores, thus saving everyone from the possibility of a human error when dealing with numbers.

Government

Machine learning is being integrated into government institutions to improve services by mining through insights (SAS Analytics, n.d.). Using machine learning in government also aids in preventing fraud.

Benefits of Machine Learning

Machine learning has become quite prominent in many industries. With its ability to classify or predict from the information given, it is a valuable source for businesses, and for the public, it is a great way to improve the interface of online applications that we generally use. Below I will list a few ways that machine learning can be integrated into various industries.

The Virtual World

Many virtual assistants like Siri, Alexa, or Bixby are run using machine learning. These systems are loaded with a database that is continuously being updated and they further learn through each person's individual input. The more these assistants learn about you, the better they work for you.

Utilities/Electricity and Water

Integrating machine learning will provide insight into the use of utilities, which will allow utility companies to accurately understand the supply and demand of the services and products they are providing. Through understanding the supply and demand, they will be able to make better decisions regarding their resources, which will most likely influence the prices.

According to Greenbird (2020), machine learning can help utility companies by identifying weaknesses in the grid, detecting unusual meter activity, and predicting outages as well as consumption. With these insights, utility services can become even more streamlined and tailored to the consumers. This means that you'll receive better services!

Manufacturing

Much like Unimate helped General Motors and other automobile companies in the 60s, introducing machine learning into the manufacturing sector will allow for a few things to happen: workers safety will be improved, production will match to sales so there's less waste, and you will save money by ensuring that you maintain your equipment as needed. Manufacturers are also able to detect defects with a higher degree of accuracy by using automated quality checks (Columbus, 2018), which means that you're less likely to receive or send a defective product out.

Retail

There are a variety of benefits of using machine learning within the retail sector. These include but are not limited to:

- Prediction of best sales combinations. Using algorithms like the apriori algorithm can help you determine which combinations of goods will increase revenue. The data revealed from this can also help you in making better pricing decisions.
- Using computer vision can help customers narrow down searches much quicker than if they were to type keywords for the item. Over time, the system will learn to better determine what could be recommended to the customer should they not want the item. A great example of this is Takealot's "Other people bought this" which shows you similar or complementary items to the one you are looking at.
- Machine learning can be used to keep track of your stock and give you insights into what you are using and how often. This is especially relevant if your retail business includes a service with it.
- Retail stores with an online presence can make the most of machine learning because they will

be able to see insights into what their customers like, view, and are saying about the product. This enables them to tailor their branding and marketing to be more enticing for their target market.

Education

Machine learning has been brought into the eLearning sphere. According to Neelakandan (2019), the benefits of including machine learning in education include:

- Creating content for learners and students that are better suited to the level that they are on instead of forcing everyone to be at the same level. This will be superb for teachers because learners or students will receive differentiated instruction that can actually help them progress at their own pace. Learning at your own pace is far healthier and better for your mental health than the stress of having to keep up is.
- Chatbots can be used to answer common questions that students have. This is great, especially with larger classes. Should students wish to know more, then they can schedule an appointment with the teacher or lecturer for additional information. Chatbots will not only benefit the learners by providing instant responses but will also lessen the load on the teacher's side because they will be able to respond to actual problems instead of mundane queries.

- Personalized learning content can motivate students or learners to perform better because the content will be directed at them instead of being generic. Generic content can feel impersonal, especially when given in an online setting. Given the outbreak of COVID19, keeping students and learners motivated to be disciplined in their approach to academics is difficult. When contact classes resume, personalized content will still be great for learners and students because it will be a more authentic experience for them. If it's too easy, you end up losing their attention and if it's too hard, you end up frustrating them, so machine learning helping teachers find the middle ground for each student will be an improvement over the generic methods that are currently employed.
- Machine learning will be able to tailor assessments to suit the level of learners and students, which can significantly boost their confidence levels and provide teachers with a better idea of which learners need more attention. When combined with differentiated instruction, tailored assessments will provide the necessary information for teachers to support and encourage learners and students more effectively. Educated youth makes for a better future for generations to come.

What's the future of machine learning?

Machine learning is becoming a massive part of our daily lives. More so than it already is. The machine learning market is expected to have grown by about 7 billion USD by 2022 due to the influx of machine learning-driven solutions (Rose, 2020). Unsupervised algorithms will improve the more machine learning is utilized, which will allow machine learning to become adept at aiding us. Computation capabilities will also increase as quantum computing advances. Quantum computers mean that there will be a great increase in the computing performance, which can enable us to test algorithms that use bigger batches of data and create more correlations.

The advent of machine learning will signal extreme personalization of our digital spaces — the content that we are exposed to will be directly targeted at you depending on the kind of content you peruse.

The integration and augmentation of machine learning are set to make our lives easier as we know it. The ability of machine learning algorithms to analyze and make mostly accurate predictions, based on the data that is fed to it, will make repetitive tasks easier and more manageable. No longer will you have to dread completing repetitive and brain-draining tasks.

Robots that are powered with machine learning are also on the horizon because they will be able to use their NLP and speech recognition to understand commands and carry them out. In addition to this, it is believed that robots will be able to carry out tasks that are dangerous or detrimental to humans (Polly, 2020). These tasks include, but are not limited to, tasks like using meat cutting machines, disabling bombs, or working with dangerous chemicals.

If you are interested in learning about machine learning or even pursuing a career in it, then there are various avenues that you can go through. Look at some of the options you have below:

Short courses

Online short courses can be taken from institutes like Simplilearn, or you can do one through various universities or colleges. For instance, the London School of Economics and Political Sciences offers a short 8-week long course on the practical applications of machine learning.

There are many institutes that offer similar short courses for beginners or as a way to enhance the skills of a graduate. Due to the popularity of machine learning applications, learning more about them and how they can be used will give you an upper hand irrespective of the field you're in.

Careers or jobs.

For the most part, to get into machine learning, you will have to get a computer science degree and then specialize in machine learning. Below are a few of the jobs that you can do once you have specialized in machine learning.

Machine learning engineers

Machine learning engineers are tasked with using the data that data scientists define and 'scaling them out to production-level models' (Zola & Zola, 2020) so that the data can be used and machine learning can take place.

Research scientist (specializing in ML)

You can enter into the world of academia and add content and value to the subdiscipline of machine learning. Your contributions could be part of later innovations.

In summary

This chapter has dealt with machine learning in-depth. We have looked at the various types of machine learning algorithms there are and outlined where they can be used. We have also taken a glance at the history of machine learning to show that we have indeed come far in our advancements of machine learning. Furthermore, places, where you can find machine learning in your daily life, were described as well as the benefits of machine learning. Lastly, we looked at what the future of machine learning might look like. Although we cannot clearly predict the future, we can make some presumptions based on the information we have. Machine learning is going to be with us for a long time and it is going to permeate our lives even more so than it is currently doing.

"Information is the oil of the 21st century, and analytics is the combustion engine" — Peter Sondergaard

Chapter 3: Big Data and Big Data Analytics

Big Data

When thinking about how to explain Big Data, I really had to think about how to frame it so that it is simple enough to understand without losing you in all the mathematics and possible jargon. In this chapter, I would like to delve into what Big Data is and how it can be analyzed. Big Data analytics is the branch that deals with analyzing and understanding the trends within datasets. The various branches of Big Data analytics will be explained before we do some time-travelling as we look at the history of Big Data. No chapter would be complete without examples showing how these technologies are being used so that is addressed at the end of the chapter before we look at the future of Big Data.

Big Data is exactly what its name infers — it is large amounts of data that cannot be analyzed by traditional methods of computing. Every time you take a photo, create content, or post online, you are creating data about yourself that can be used. There are billions of people on social media — if each person is using social media as much (or as little) as you are, how much data do you think is being collected?

Within the framework of artificial intelligence, Big Data is important because it is what 'powers' artificial intelligence. Machine learning systems, symbolic systems, and deep learning systems all need data in order to be 'taught' or programmed efficiently and sufficiently for use. Without Big Data, we would not be able to train the numerous AI systems that are making our lives easier.

Imagine that you want to open a big restaurant. Before designing your menu, you want to find out what kind of cuisine the locals eat. If you only ask 10 of the 1000 people what they would like to eat, then the statistics received would not reflect the desires of the locals but only that of a minority. Similarly, without accurately analyzing Big Data, AI systems would be skewed. An example of this is the issue that Google search engines had a few years back: when someone typed 'professional hairstyles' into the search bar, the results that came back showed images of Caucasian people. Where else if you searched for 'unprofessional hairstyles' then the top images were of people of color wearing their natural hair. Of course, this does not indicate that Google or its algorithms are inherently racist, but it does provide a perfect example of how results can be skewed if ample samples of data are not available.

Saying that Big Data is just a large dataset is vague and ambiguous because it raised a lot of other questions: How big is big? Is the size the only thing that characterizes Big Data? The answer to your questions is that not all data can be considered 'Big Data.' In order for datasets to be classified as Big Data, it needs to have a few characteristics.

The traditional characteristics that a dataset should have in order to be deemed 'Big Data' are the three Vs of Big Data, according to Gartner. Gartner is an Information Technology company that is "a global research and advisory firm [that provides] information, advice, and tools for leaders" (Wikipedia contributors, 2021c) in various industries. These three Vs are volume, velocity, and variety (Oracle, n.d.).

In short, Big Data is only considered as Big Data when there is a massive amount of it (volume) that cannot be processed by ordinary means. It also needs to be generated quickly (velocity) and have many types (variety) of data. Once the dataset has met this criterion, it can then be considered Big Data.

A great example of Big Data is the data that Facebook collects. There are approximately 2.8 billion users on Facebook and there are about 350 million images alone that are uploaded every day! Facebook is a medium that also allows for videos and texts to be uploaded so the amount of data that can be found on Facebook's servers is massive. As you can see, the data from Facebook follows Gartner's three V's — it is voluminous, has variety, and generated quickly.

But having all of this data stored serves no point if it's not being analyzed. Otherwise, it's just raw data with no use, and that's where Big Data analytics comes in. To deal with these massive amounts of data, we have data scientists who use something called Big Data analytics.

What is Big Data Analytics?

Big Data analytics is the use of 'advanced analytic techniques' (IBM, n.d.-a) for large sets of data. As explained previously, Big Data simply cannot be processed by using traditional methods of computing. Being able to process these large amounts of data is important because it allows us to understand patterns within the dataset. These patterns have the ability to give us insights that can influence many decisions. Currently, Big Data analytics is being used for commercial purposes, but it does have the ability to be used to make decisions that actually better the lives of people. For example, a company called SocialCops used Big Data analytics in India to decide where to place LPG stations so that people could easily access better fuel sources (TEDx Talks, 2017).

Big Data analytics are performed by data analysts. They collect data from a wide range of sources which include, but are not limited to:

- data from the adverts on the internet: every time you click on an advert to view it, you are providing analysts with information on your possible interests and potential interests.
- webserver logs: these are lists of your interactions on a specific website. This allows analysts to look at your behavior on the application.
- application history: your application history shows analysts what kind of applications you use and provides information in a similar manner to web server logs. Naturally, due to the fact that applications are usually geared towards a certain goal, each application's history will show some different aspects of your behavior.
- all social media uploads, downloads, and interactions: this data is essentially used to profile you individually.
- data from sensors: this data includes videos, images, etc. of the world in real-time that is

then translated to a digital format (Iota Communications, Inc., 2020).

In the simplest terms: once this data is collected, it can then be processed. To be processed, the data must be configured so that it can be analyzed with ease. Once processed, the data is reviewed for veracity and quality. This means that the analysts look for errors, which can include duplicates or formatting errors. Once the data is processed and quality checked, an algorithm is applied to the data to 'derive insights' and look for meaningful correlations (Monnappa, 2021).

For a deeper understanding of Big Data analytics, let's look at its life cycle in-depth.

1. Business evaluation – the reason for analyzing the data is made clear. This ensures that the correct algorithms are used to collect data that is relevant.
2. Identifying the data – now that we understand what we want to do with the data, we can then decide what data is needed. For instance, if we had a mobile network company and wanted to know when most people make phone calls to determine 'peak times' then we would not need information on when people send text messages.
3. Filtering through the data – we are dealing with a lot of data and sometimes that data can become corrupted. Corrupted data will mess

with the patterns that you are trying to find in the datasets.

4. Pulling out the data – once you've made sure that your data is 'pure,' you can then begin to extract the data. Data needs to be compatible with the tool being used so, if it isn't, then it's transformed into a compatible format so it can be analyzed.
5. Data aggregation – basically, data is gathered from various sources and then a summary is created.
6. Analysis – whew! Data is finally analyzed, and other types of tools are used to discover information within the statistics given.
7. Visualization – wouldn't you agree that it's so much better to look at an image than it is to look at a table of statistics? Once the data is analyzed, tools like Tableau are used to produce visualizations of the analysis.
8. Data is made available – stakeholders within the business are given the data so that they can make informed decisions.

This is the basic life cycle of data analytics. However, data analytics can be further explained in terms of its purpose, there are 4 types and each type is used for a specific purpose.

Descriptive Analytics

Descriptive analytics is when analysts take old data and put it into a form that people can easily read (Simplilearn, 2021). This includes forms like using an infographic or a graphic visualization. Descriptive analytics is particularly useful for providing solutions to problems that have been experienced or for providing the rationale for why a certain decision is being made.

Descriptive analytics essentially allows people who are non-technical to understand that data so informed decisions can take place. Descriptive analytics essentially answers the question "what happened" when looking at data trends. Descriptive analytics is most often used in the commercial sector because it provides a really neat overview of everything that has happened.

However, you can see the applications of descriptive analytics when you look at any sort of graphic illustration of statistics that come from companies that interact with large sets of data. For example, if you create a Facebook page, you will be able to see insights, which will include how many people viewed the page, how many people you've reached, how many times posts have been engaged with, and many other different statistics. These statistics give you an overview of how well your page is doing and the insights can provide you information so that you can improve either specific elements or holistically. In the age of digital media, descriptive analytics being available on social media is great.

Diagnostic Analytics

Diagnostic analytics is done to troubleshoot so that businesses can see or infer what caused the problem or change. The question that diagnostic analytics answer is "why did it happen?"

When looking at the data by using a diagnostic analysis, it is typically done when there are problems instead of trying to see past patterns. When looking to diagnose the issue, we look for three elements: identifying anomalies, looking at the analytics to determine patterns, and show causal relationships (Walker, 2018).

These three elements usually provide an indication as to why we are facing the issue that we are facing.

Predictive Analytics

Predictive analytics looks at both past and present data to make a prediction. Predictive analytics is typically used in the commercial sector so that the businesses can see customer trends, which can be analyzed. Through these analyzes, companies will make decisions to improve their products, services, or reach.

But predictive analytics can also be used in other sectors like education or government. Looking at trends within institutes provides us with the necessary insight to understand whether there is a need to revisit policies or make other changes. Predictive analytics in the government and education sector can potentially make decisions easier to make because predictive analytics typically provides the statistical evidence to support the prediction.

Prescriptive Analytics

Prescriptive analytics is one of the main forms of analytics that helps with decision-making. However, unlike other analytics, it provides a decision rather than providing data that you make a decision on. Predictive analytics combines both descriptive and predictive analytics because you need to understand both past and present trends in order to make a good decision.

Prescriptive analytics can be broken into two different approaches — it can either make a decision through optimization or it can use computational logic. Optimization looks at every angle of the data as outlined by the business where else the computational logic takes pre-existing business knowledge. Computational logic is great for simple choices that are not dynamic while optimization is great for more complex decisions.

As you can see, data analytics can be looked at from various perspectives depending on what kind of information we want to extract from the data. Now that you have an understanding of how data can be analyzed, I would like to delve into the history of Big Data so that you can understand just how far we've come from being able to know that there are large amounts of data being unanalyzed to actually using Big Data to inform decisions.

History of Big Data

Big Data analytics is based on the usage of statistics. To understand the history of Big Data, you need to understand a little bit of the history of when statistics officially became part of Big Data.

1663: Statistics is founded in relation to Big Data.

John Graunt was an English statistician who conducted the first statistics-based experiment in hospitals where he theorized that, with enough data, he would be able to create an 'early warning' system for people who were afflicted with the bubonic plague.

1865: The concept of Business Intelligence.

Richard Millar Devens is credited with the term 'business intelligence' because he used it in his book 'Cyclopaedia of Commercial and Business Anecdotes' in 1865 to explain how a banker became successful by collecting information from his market and utilizing it to his advantage. It was one of the first recognitions of 'Big Data' being used, albeit through mechanical means.

1880: Storing and sorting system created.

One of the biggest issues with Big Data is not the availability but, rather, the inability to store it and subsequently process it. In 1880, statistician and businessman Herman Hollerith created a system that helped summarize large amounts of information. The system is called the Herman Hollerith Tabulating Machine and was created to solve the issue of the 1880 US census having too much data to record and analyze.

A few years prior, Joseph Marie Jacquard invented and used a system of punched holes in different formations to instruct a machine to weave different patterns. Charles Babbage tried to adapt this system and create a steam-powered information processor. Unfortunately, he was never able to create it. However, this creation provided Herman Hollerith with inspiration and he proceeded to create the Herman Hollerith Tabulating Machine, which worked by holding a single person's data on one sheet of paper. To record this data, the clerks would punch in the details of the citizen and the machine would then 'file' it away. Once 'filed', the results were then registered on a counter board through electromechanical means. By adjusting the wires on the machine, people were able to understand the information in new ways.

1928: Information storage changes

Fritz Pfleumer invented the magnetic tape that could be used for storing information. Initially, the tape could only store music, but, by the 1950s, it was able to store other information. This method revolutionized the world of data storage and is still used today for some information.

1965: First data center created to store tax returns.

In 1965, the United States decided to build a data center to store the 742 million tax returns along with over 175 million records of fingerprints. Unfortunately, the data center did not reach completion because there was fear that the information could be used incorrectly (Rijmenam, 2021).

1970: Invents relational model for database management

Computer scientist Edgar F. Codd created a relational model for databases and management systems. Essentially this allowed people to easily find information in databases without having to first understand the inner workings of the database. Imagine how tiresome it would be if you had to understand and navigate algorithms every time you wanted to search for information on Google? Edgar's invention provided companies with a means of classifying 'Big Data' and then retrieving relevant information. You only needed to know what to look for instead of how to look for it.

1989: Term 'Big Data' is coined

Based on the understanding of what Big Data is, we are able to see that Big Data was always around—the term Big Data was just not used. Author Erik Larson wrote an article that stated 'the keepers of Big Data say they are doing it for the consumer's benefit. But data has a way of being used for purposes other than originally intended" (World Economic Forum, 2015) which is deemed as one of the first mentions of 'Big Data' as a term.

1997: How much information is in the world?

A paper titled "How much information is there in the world" was published and it theorized that there could be 12,000 petabytes of data. To show that this number is not insane, he uses the quickly expanding web as an example. He further explains that, though this data is 'collected,' there is no way to analyze it, which renders it useless.

1999: 'Big Data' as we know it

By 1999, researchers were using the term Big Data to describe the vast amounts of data that were available. Unfortunately, there was still no way for it to be sufficiently analyzed.

2001: Big Data is defined.

Doug Laney, an analyst at Gartner, defines three of the characteristics of Big Data. These three characteristics are volume, velocity, and variety.

2005: Web size increases and Big Data framework introduced.

The worldwide web, which previously had mostly service providers providing data, was expanded and allowed users to generate their own content which increased the amount of overall raw data available.

A framework called Hadoop was created for the storage and analysis of Big Data sets and its ability to manage unstructured data was a bonus for data analysts.

2006: current Big Data rises

Through the years more and more data has been accumulated and created, and many other frameworks to sort through this data are created as a result.

2011: Data scientists are sorely needed.

In 2011, it was estimated that the United States would need between 140,000 and 190,000 professional data scientists in order to address issues such as privacy, security, and use of intellectual property. These ethical issues would need to be addressed and resolved by data scientists before Big Data could be fully used in society.

As you can see, Big Data isn't something novel — it has been around since the beginning of time, and what characterizes it has changed based on the amounts of data that are created. In the 1800s, the Herman Hollerith machine was a prime example of a system that could 'compute' large amounts of data. Prior to the Herman Hollerith machine, such large data could not be computed by using the 'traditional methods' available at that time.

2017: Application of Big Data in various industries

There are numerous applications of Big Data that are being developed in the hopes of creating a better environment. Some of these developments include:

1. Increasing safety by analyzing data and looking at a prediction of what crime will be.
2. Using data science algorithms to predict whether a person would have a second heart attack.

These are just two of the ways in which Big Data made a big impact in two industries.

Currently: Continued application with ethical concerns

Big Data is being analyzed and used by massive corporations, but there have been many ethical concerns that have arisen from the use of Big Data analytics. One such incident that you may be aware of came in the form of WhatsApp changing its policy and stating that it would be collecting data, which sparked a massive shift from WhatsApp to other applications that were deemed 'less intrusive,' such as Telegram and Signal.

Examples of Big Data

Big Data can be found everywhere. Big Data is simply large amounts of data — it is only made 'functional' when it is analyzed. There are many industries that are making use of Big Data analytics. Whenever we think about Big Data analytics, we typically think about the commercial sector, but it has been, and is being used in, a variety of other industries. This section of the chapter will serve to highlight the places where Big Data analytics is used.

Targeted marketing

By using the information gleaned from consumer data, businesses are able to tailor their advertisements, and even products, so that they are made more appealing to their target market. The more appealing their product or service, the more sales they generate.

Risk management

Because Big Data analytics is a great way to find information, it can easily be used to determine how much of a risk a new decision could be. This is helpful in many spheres aside from commerce. Non-profit organizations will be able to utilize the derived meaning from data to see if their approaches will work, or if they will be able to provide concrete predictions for the success of their project.

Hopefully, at a later stage, Big Data and AI will be able to have personalized risk management freely available for the public. This could help potential students determine the success of the careers that they may want to choose, which in turn can help the economy.

Maintenance

Using Big Data will be able to help you maintain your company's equipment and can predict when you should do things like inventory management, manage supplier networks, or notify personnel about potential delays.

For the general public, this information can be useful for people who want to buy new items. For example, people who would like to buy cars will be able to access statistics on how the car works and lasts. It can also provide them with information on how long before parts need to be replaced or checked to prevent accidents.

Education

Big Data is shaping the way that we look at things within the education system. By using Big Data within the education sector, we will be able to improve the way that we teach, as well as the content that is taught. The use of Big Data analytics will provide means to predict student performance as well as provide solutions to the problems that students face. Not only will this help the students but it will also help the educators because they will not need to manually search for this information.

Police Services

Although it may seem surprising, many police departments are including Big Data analytics and machine learning because it provides them with information that they would otherwise miss. An example of this is the application ShotSpotter, which collects sound information and then uses descriptive analytics to display the data so that the police department can interpret the data (Willems, 2017).

Health Care

Health care systems are digitizing patient records and through predictive data analytics, they are able to determine which groups are more statistically prone to certain diseases, allergies, or maladies. This information combined with what is already on record for the patient can augment doctor's abilities to diagnose their patients. Using Big Data analytics also made sure that the data being captured and analyzed is not corrupted or duplicated.

One of the biggest uses for Big Data analytics within the healthcare system is using it to help cure cancer. Big Data analytics in cancer treatments and identification are still in progress but there has been remarkable progress. It is through the use of Big Data analytics they found that "Desipramine works as an antidepressant for some lung cancers" (Willems, 2017).

Entertainment Industry

Although it seems strange to talk about Big Data analytics in the entertainment industry, the use of Big Data analytics is surprisingly common when roles are cast, and new shows are created. Predictive and descriptive analytics are used to determine whether the show will garner good publicity based on the show's content and the actors. Actors are even affected by these factors because their popularity (or lack thereof) can even be part of the overall decision process on whether they will get the job.

Cyberspace

This seems like a no-brainer considering all that you've learned so far, but did you know that Big Data analytics can influence you through targeted marketing? In 2018, Big Data analytics from Facebook was obtained illegally and was used to influence the decisions of thousands of voters in the USA. This is just one example of Big Data being used in cyberspace for reasons other than commercial reasons.

What's the future of Big Data?

Analyzing Big Data is still a largely underdeveloped field. Due to the sheer masses of data that are available, we find ourselves unable to use even the currently advanced computational methods to analyze all the Big Data that we have access to. In order to accurately analyze Big Data, one needs to group it into sets and then analyze a large data set instead of all of it. However, this may change in the near future as scientists are working on creating quantum computers that will have the ability to compute Big Data easily. Whatever happens, we know that Big Data is here to stay.

The future of Big Data

According to Internet of Things expert Khvoynitskaya (2020), there are a few predictions for the next few years.

1. Data being stored in clouds will continue and increase. Most people already have various clouds that are used to store your data. These clouds include Google Drive, iCloud, and OneDrive.
    a. Previously, businesses needed to have their own data centers if they had data-heavy applications, but cloud storage is changing that.
    b. There are two different types of clouds: public clouds and private clouds. Public clouds are available to anyone in the general public while private clouds only have one organization's data within it.
2. Machine learning will become better because of the abundance of Big Data. Remember, Big Data drives AI and machine learning because it provides the systems with the input for it to learn. A great example of a huge database is ImageNet.
3. There will be an increase in demand for data scientists and chief data officers. According to a survey done by KPMG, one of the top skills that is scarce is Big Data analytics.

4. There will be a few issues around Big Data: one of them being privacy. As the amount of data grows and evolves the abilities of AI and machine learning, there is also an evolution of malicious spyware among other cyberattacks. The use of Big Data for analytics will also force institutes to safeguard their data with more ferocity.

Understanding how Big Data is going to influence our future everyday lives is vital so that we can prepare for it. If you are interested in Big Data and would like to pursue a career in it, or even just learn more about it, then below is a list of things you can do to get into Big Data.

Short courses:

These are the following places that offer Big Data related short courses:

Udemy: Udemy is completely online and allows you to work at your own pace for the most part. They also frequently have sales so you can pick up these courses for much cheaper if you watch their website for sales.

Coursera: Coursera is like Udemy and is completely online. Coursera also has many short courses that are accredited by universities and colleges — these courses will expect you to work according to a schedule and is a lot more structured than most courses in UDemy.

Universities and colleges: With the appearance of COVID-19, much more has migrated online and there are numerous universities and colleges that offer short online courses. To find out what is offered, you will need to visit the institute's website.

Careers or jobs

If you've decided that you would like to pursue a career in Big Data, then there are many different fields that you can go into. Below I will list the various jobs that you can do. Big Data is the umbrella term for what you will be working with — similar to how people study medicine and can become different types of doctors.

Big Data Engineer

A Big Data engineer is a person who creates and/or manages Big Data infrastructure (Toptal, n.d.). Oftentimes, a Big Data engineer's role can get crossed with that of a Big Data scientist, but the two are fundamentally different. The Big Data engineer is simply in charge of the system while the data scientist will work with the algorithms and statistics that provide the backbone for the engineer's creation.

Data Architect

A data architect is like a designer for companies' Big Data. The data architect creates programs for the company that is based on their goals (Olavsrud, 2020). For example, if a company wanted to know how many people are using product A vs product B, the data architect would create a system that would collect that specific information for analyzing.

Data Warehouse Manager

Data warehouse managers are the people that oversee the warehouses that store all the data. In addition to monitoring the storage of this data, they are also in charge of ensuring that each department's data is stored in the correct place for later retrieval (*Data Warehouse Manager Salary | PayScale*, n.d.).

Database Manager

Much like the name alludes, a database manager is a person that manages the data itself. These managers look at the trends and are able to determine whether something should be scaled up or needs maintenance (*Database Manager Job Description*, 2018).

Business Intelligence analyst

Although this does not have data or Big Data anywhere in its title, business intelligence analysts use Big Data to determine the choices that a business should collect in order to make decisions that will be beneficial for the business. Essentially, they "transform data into insights that drive business value" (White, 2019).

Data Scientist

Data scientists deal with the raw, unprocessed Big Data and they process, analyze, and derive meaning from the data. The data scientist typically works with data that is unstructured and makes sense of it.

Data Modeler

Data modelers are the people who design complex systems that will allow your traditional computer to 'understand' the Big Data. Essentially, the data modeler works with a data architect and together they build a system that can easily be used by non-technical people. Can you just imagine if you had to call a technician out every time you wanted to know how your business is doing? That would increase your expenditure a lot!

Database Developer

Database developers, or database programmers, are the people who create and ensure that programs are efficient for the purpose they are designed — collecting and analyzing Big Data in the way that the company needs it. A company that wants to understand the sales statistics of their shoes doesn't need to have the sale of their accessories added to the same program. Database developers are also in charge of any type of large maintenance on the system.

Database administrator

The database administrator is the person in charge of using the programs that the developers, scientists, modeler, and engineers have created. Their job is to ensure that the people who need to access the database are able to, and those that shouldn't are unable to access it.

Data analyst

The name says it all — these are the people that analyze the results and can then provide feedback based on the statistics picked up.

In summary

In this chapter we explored Big Data, its history, examples of its implementation, and the various places or jobs that you can get into if you have an interest in Big Data. Big Data is an amazing field if you are a person that loves statistics and finding patterns. By going into any job in Big Data, you will be dealing with statistics and various patterns of behavior. However, the best part about dealing with these statistics and patterns is that they all have real-world relevance. When you find out that more men like coffee than women, it isn't based on a small pool of data, but, rather, a huge amount of data which makes it closer to being true. Aside from being able to help the businesses gain insight, these statistics can also help you gain insights into people's habits, which is always interesting from a social point of view. Knowledge is power, which means that the more you know the better you can prepare for change or to create it.

Chapter 4: Bringing it all together.

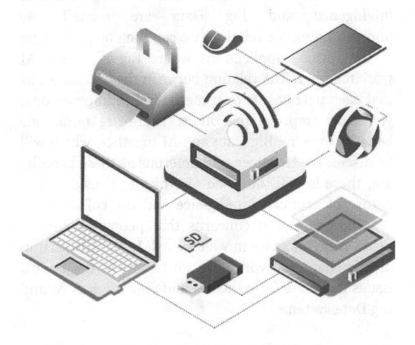

Previously we discussed each individual element: Big Data, AI, and its sub-discipline machine learning. But, how do those things work together? Are they even related? Yes! There is a largely symbiotic relationship between the two elements.

AI is the umbrella term for systems that can mimic aspects of a human's intelligence, but it further breaks into various components. Big Data is not actually part of AI, but it provides the fodder for AI. Without Big

Data and Big Data analytics, AI would be vastly undertrained and underutilized. In the simplest words: Big Data drives all components of artificial intelligence.

In this chapter, we will look at how artificial intelligence and Big Data are related. By understanding the relation, we can then begin looking at the various applications where Big Data and AI work together. The relation between the two shows us that each part has its own merit, and to improve one, you must improve the other. There are numerous benefits to using Big Data and AI together, which will be discussed. However, as numerous as these benefits are, there is still the issue of ethics to consider. The nature of artificial intelligence and the collection of Big Data raise key concerns that people should be made aware of as we move forward. In the last section of this chapter, I will delve into some of the ethical issues that arise from the use and regulation of AI and Big Data systems.

AI and Big Data: The relation

Artificial Intelligence is a broad field which includes symbolic learning and machine learning. Both sub-disciplines of AI use Big Data to get better at whatever it's been tasked to do, and AI's algorithms help analyze Big Data. Without artificial intelligence, we would find it difficult to analyze Big Datasets which would lead to insights that are fragmented from the whole picture. Where else, without Big Data, we would not be able to make the progress that we are currently making in artificial intelligence. Below, I will explain some of the ways in which AI and Big Data work together.

1. Artificial Intelligence algorithms make it increasingly more possible to analyze Big Data.

   AI is able to sieve through all the information that is fed to it and can provide insights into the information that is fed into it. As we ask more questions about the data, we are able to redesign algorithms to find those patterns to provide answers. As the need to find out new information arises, algorithms will be created or redefined so that the information can be mined from the data. Data-driven decisions will become the norm as we continue using Big Data and AI.

2. Data analytics become easier with AI.

If any of you are interested in going into data science, then the great news is that you will be able to analyze data easily and quickly by using AI systems. Not only will these systems make your jobs easier, but as the systems become better at their jobs, data scientists will no longer need to complete 'mundane' tasks but will be needed to check that the systems are sieving through the data correctly.

3. Big Data will allow AI to progress at an even faster rate.

    The success of AI subdisciplines, like natural language processing, will progress much faster where Big Data is able to be processed and fed to systems in a way that they can compute. As mentioned earlier, the advent of quantum computing may catapult the field of AI to new heights.

4. AI systems can be even more useful than they are.

    With Big Data powering the learning pace of AI systems, we will be able to personalize and utilize our assistants with even more ease and efficiency. These advanced AI systems will not be limited to assistants on our phones, laptops, or smart devices, but they will extend into our daily commutes and perhaps even into our personal lives. Imagine having a robotic assistant to help with morning chores and reminders so you never run late or forget stuff again?

Examples of AI and Big Data in use

There are many industries that are using a combination of AI and Big Data to improve their business models and products. Some of these include the automobile industry, various retailers, energy companies, and the financial sector to name a few.

Automobile industry

The advent of the self-driving car is nearly upon us. For the self-driving car to become a reality, it needs to be able to use Big Data and various elements of AI.

It would need Big Data to understand the trends of the roads — for instance, at 8 am most main roads will be filled with traffic — it would need AI and machine learning to drive without hitting anything or endangering the person inside of the car.

Aside from the self-driving car, automobile industries are also using this combination of technologies to drive their production and marketing to increase sales.

Commerce

Companies like Coca-Cola and Heineken are using these technologies to increase their sales and production. Some of these giants are also using AI augmentation, which is basically when they use AI systems to help improve the work a human is doing instead of replacing the human. There is also a huge boom in using AI and Big Data in the ECommerce industry. Within the ECommerce industry, you can find examples of AI and Big Data being used.

- Companies are using predictive analytics and machine learning to boost sales by micro-targeting people.
- E-Companies are becoming more user-friendly as they integrate functions like voice-to-text within their applications so that even the barely literate are able to use their services. The addition of the voice-to-text function also enables your microphone, which can sometimes pick up what you're saying when the application is not in use. This 'listening' can influence what your recommended or suggested products look like.
- By implementing Big Data analytics and machine learning in e-companies, they are able to make purchasing on their site safer. The combination of AI and Big Data will allow the system to create an alert if there is suspicious activity.

Energy sector

Energy companies are using these systems to improve their services and sustainability of the energy that they are providing. Currently, the leader in this is the company BP, which has integrated these systems into their company (Marr, 2018).

There are various start-ups that are using Big Data and AI in applications to monitor, manage, and improve energy usage. According to StartUs Insights, a data science company with endorsements from Samsung and Nestle, there are five top applications using Big Data and AI in the energy sector (2019). These applications are:

- Currant: This application allows customers to improve energy consumption based on their patterns. Currant has a line of smart home products which allow people to control their home remotely. This means that there is no longer a need to leave lights on because you know you'll be coming home late — instead, you can simply switch your lights on remotely. This way you save energy and are able to control how your home uses energy. The data that the Currant application receives is prescriptively analyzed so that each user can get personalized suggestions on how to conserve energy.

- Spark Cognition: This application allows energy companies to maintain their machinery. The AI systems are able to inspect the machinery and alert operators of potential failure.
- VIA: VIA is a start-up that makes use of predictive analytics. It analyzes information about the consumption, outages, and the amount of energy generated by renewable sources such as the wind. By using these massive sets of data, VIA is able to predict how companies can better distribute their energy and prevent outages.
- Ambyint: This application combines AI and Big Data analytics to ensure that the time used to search for oil wells is minimized, but production is maximized by using something akin to drones to search.
- Raptor Maps: Raptor Maps uses drones to collect masses of data through virtual inspections of renewable energy systems.

These are just five of the hundreds of other ways that energy companies are integrating Big Data and AI into their infrastructure.

Financial Sector

This sector arguably has one of the biggest data sets that it has to deal with because it includes every transaction that is made, which needs to be allocated to a person, and then that person's 'pattern' has to be looked at determining whether they qualify for things like loans and lower premiums. With the massive amounts of data that they have to deal with, implementing a combination of AI, machine learning, and Big Data analytics would have ensured that the company does better and can more accurately serve their customers. Big Data and AI work together in the financial sector in the following places: risk management, fraud detection, and customer happiness.

Risk detection and management: Banks are employing predictive data analytics so that they can detect and manage risks with greater efficiency. In order to detect risks and subsequently manage them, the AI systems would need to be fed with the Big Data that is collected. One of the risks that banks would want to monitor includes whether a person will pay back a loan. Through using data analytics, banks are able to predict whether a person is likely to pay back a loan based on their previous transactions. Once they have a data-driven prediction, they can then create contingency plans.

Fraud detection: Detecting fraud early means that you minimize risks. Big Data analytics allows you to monitor activity and raises red flags when suspicious activity is detected. Information that the financial sector collects includes your zip codes, travel patterns, income levels, age, and the place where you live. All of these factors dictate what you should be able to buy and provides a general idea of how you spend your money. When this information is fed into the AI system, the system will be able to track anomalies. For example, it is unlikely that you would be able to afford a Ferrari if you earn minimum wage, live in a poor area, divert half of your income to student loans and have dependents. Naturally, if you bought a Ferrari under those circumstances, it would be suspicious, and you would be investigated. Other areas of fraud include activity on your account from an unusual place — for example, an online transaction from a different part of the country.

<u>Customer happiness:</u> Within the financial sector, the happiness of the customers is dealt with in different ways — in most banks, chatbots are used so that customers can get immediate feedback about their queries. Within the financial sector, they also collect data in the form of satisfaction surveys, which leads to better services.

Healthcare

The advent of Big Data and artificial intelligence being used in the healthcare system has provided amazing opportunities for growth and the improvement of all who use the health care system.

- Using Big Data and artificial intelligence means that the government can make better decisions about the strategic plans of the town. For example, by analyzing the number of people in a specific area and understanding the health statuses of the people in that area will provide ample grounds for an additional health facility to be built. This can also ensure that hospitals have an idea of what possible trends could be seen. For instance, during COVID-19, understanding how people lived in an area gave an indication of how quickly the virus would spread. The virus would spread with greater velocity if the area is overly congested. Similarly, you can also determine what kind of resources you will need should you see someone from that area in the hospital.

- Telemedicine is using technology to provide diagnosis and medication. This feat has been made quite easy with the wide range of data that is able to be processed, as well as the fact that smartphones and wearable devices are popular.
- Electronic files where important information is available in a central database allow for doctors to keep track of patients, allows for fraudulent activities to be tracked, and also ensures that new doctor-patient relationships are made easier. The doctor will already have the most important information on file so there will be less scope for human error to rear its head.

Fitness

Big Data is used in fitness applications to crunch your data and cheer you on so that you can reach your goals. Big Data is used so that you can be grouped with like-health people and your progress can be as accurate as possible. Examples of this include Samsung Health, Huawei Health, and Google Fit to name a few.

These are some of the applications of Big Data and AI — you most likely recognize and even use some of them. Applications like Samsung Health help you keep track of your overall health and even encourages you to do better by instructing you what to do so you can achieve your goals.

Benefits of using AI and Big Data

AI and Big Data together have a horde of benefits. They are a power couple of note that is going to change our lives as we know it. They have already started changing our lives as you recognize some of the applications that are being used. Below, I will list some of the benefits of using AI and Big Data.

1. As a consumer, you will receive better services when using AI and Big Data. Machine learning will ensure that your experience is personalized and that you can get serviced through different ways (uploading an image, using voice-to-text, using a document, etc.)

2. As someone with an E-Company or business, using AI and Big Data analytics will allow you to pander to your market more efficiently, thereby allowing your sales to increase.

3. Integrating AI and Big Data into companies and organizations will provide augmentation for the human counterparts within the organization. This augmentation will allow for personal and professional growth because there will be more time to upskill due to the assistance from AI-powered systems. Additionally, upskilling employees helps the business in the long-run

4. With all the insights from Big Data analytics, you will be able to determine the best prices, quality, and services for your customers.
5. Through using Big Data, applications using AI can be improved exponentially. For example, doctors would not need to attend to every patient immediately because an AI system could theoretically 'diagnose' a patient and move patients who need immediate attention to the front while scheduling those that do not.
6. When used by the government, important decisions can be made that could be beneficial to all.

Where to from here?

We are currently taking great strides in incorporating AI, machine learning, and Big Data into our lives. It is presumed that the computer science community will expand exponentially because there is a need for more people within the field to further the growth of AI, machine learning, and the issues that are presented with Big Data.

Decision-making is one of the things that are going to change as AI and Big Data evolve. Machine learning is already being used in businesses and data predictive, descriptive and prescriptive data analytics are employed to get consumers interested. The average person in the street does not recognize this as something that really affects him or her. However, we are already facing small changes where AI and Big Data are learning to help us with decisions. For example, on your phone, you can use a variety of applications to set goals — most smartphones have their own version of a health app or a cloud service that can be used for reaching your health goals, completing tasks, etc. These prompts are micro-transactions that help you make decisions. As technology evolves, we will be able to have much more prescriptive (and personalized) 'solutions' for the goals that we are intending on setting.

The workforce is going to change drastically with the implementation of Big Data and AI. AI systems will be able to replace people who are doing jobs that are repetitive and mundane. Jobs such as data capturing, accounting, and anything else that can be automated. Although this may seem alarming, I do not think that it will be an issue because education institutes are already integrating the skills and knowledge that are needed to ensure that you are employable in the upcoming revolution.

With Big Data and AI being melded together and producing accurate profiles of us, the best way forward is to ensure that we are constantly upskilling so that we will not be replaced by AI, and to ensure that we read the terms and conditions of the applications that we use. If you are fine with your data being shared and used, then you should be aware of how it is used so that you can spot it when you are being micro-targeted.

Ethical issues

Before we begin with what ethical issues are being faced when we speak about artificial intelligence and Big Data, I would like to give a brief definition of what ethics is. In the simplest terms, ethics is the study of what is right and wrong. We learn about ethics from various sources such as your primary caregivers, your church, your community, and the school that you attend. This ideal of what is right and what is wrong is what helps inform our decisions.

Artificial Intelligence needs Big Data to work smoothly. The data needs to be fed into the system so that it can be analyzed and learned from. But where does this Big Data come from? It's collected from people like you and me through all the applications, devices, and online services that we use. It's also collected voluntarily when we fill out surveys and quizzes. So where does ethics come in when we're discussing Big Data and AI?

Ethics comes in when we look at how AI machines are using our data. This data that is collected can be used for anything from sales to more sinister motives, like indoctrinating the youth to believe something. Big Data and AI make propaganda easy to spread. Furthermore, people's agendas can be 'pushed' by simply exposing them more than others. The combination of AI and Big Data makes profiling so easy makes what happens to our data a real ethical concern.

Terms and Conditions

Do you know that all of your data is being captured, and, to an extent, used? You probably do. Or you have this vague notion of what they are doing with your data: maybe using your location as a way to prevent fraudulent logins. But, do you really know what your data is being used for? Can you explain what your Facebook is doing with your data? Or Twitter, or

Google? You most likely can't explain in any depth what they are doing with your data. And so, we come to the first ethical issue that using Big Data and artificial intelligence bring to the forefront. What is your data being used for, and do you consent to it being used in that way? The short answer is that you give your consent the moment you accept the Ts and Cs — you simply have to trust that your data is used correctly. It is ethical to collect data, provided you have consent, and the person knows what you are going to be doing with the data. In this case, the consent is given when you accept the Ts and Cs but are you really informed on what the terms and conditions entail?

The fact that organizations do not make the terms and conditions 'user friendly' makes us wonder if they're preying on our laziness or the terms and conditions really *must be so tedious* that reading it feels like drinking a blitzed taco. Unfortunately, service providers have not created visualizations of their terms and conditions for understanding purposes. At best, you get a shortlist that says something along the lines of "the following terms have changed" but you're not told what it has been changed to unless you read the whole agreement. Most people simply accept the terms and conditions because they need to be able to use the application and, without accepting the terms of use, they would be unable to work.

Targeted marketing

The collection of your personal data doesn't seem too bad until you realize that your entire life is essentially being monitored. Have you ever noticed that you'd have a conversation about going on a holiday with a friend and then a few days later, your newsfeed has adverts for resorts and travelling? Yep, your smart devices are listening to you and they're personalizing your content. Which is great, right? You want to go on a holiday and with these recommendations, half the work is done! But, what happens when you become a mindless consumer because the content shown to you is like a drug that you must try?

The use of Big Data and AI raises another key ethical issue when it comes to their analytics: is it right to almost coerce people into buying stuff? When AI and Big Data are employed to personalize your news feed, your likes and dislikes are registered and everything that is directed at you will appeal to your likes. This is problematic because it strips you of some of your autonomy because the more you're exposed to something, the more desensitized or accepting of it you will become. AI and Big Data make it possible for you to essentially be profiled. The personalization of your content that seems so benevolent can become a way to 'brainwash' you. By brainwash, I don't mean that a beam is going to take your thoughts away and replace them with something else. I mean that your perception of things can be changed simply through being exposed to certain media over and over. For instance, data analytics taken illegally from Facebook in 2018 was used for political gain and it influenced the outcome of the voting that year.

Privacy and security

Privacy is another huge concern when it comes to ethical issues within AI and Big Data because data is powerful. Put into the wrong hands and the effects could be catastrophic. Once your data is collected, it needs to be secured in a way that will prevent people with malicious intent from accessing it. The issue that we have with this is that machine learning is constantly evolving, which means malware powered by machine learning can also evolve along with the new security features.

The next big question is are you actually in control of your own data? Because AI and Big Data are gaining insights from your data that is retrieved from all of your social media accounts, your web browser history, your location services, and many other places. What happens to the data you've already given if you decide you no longer want to accept the terms and conditions, so you delete your account? Well, according to an article from CNS News, your Facebook data is stored for a period of time before identifying information is removed and your data stored (2018). This means that once you've given your data over, it's not as easy to take it back.

Furthermore, given that our devices, like laptops and phones, are constantly listening, would AI robot assistants do the same? The 4th industrial revolution aims to provide us with this awesome technology, but who controls the information that the robots accrue? As an additional concern that is not necessarily related to privacy and security — whose set of values and ethics will these robots be programmed with? These are all questions that need to be asked and answered before we jump onto the bandwagon of integrating technology fully into our lives.

Children

It's not surprising that children are on the internet. With AI and Big Data analytics already being used on applications like Facebook where many children have accounts, we are forced to wonder about the safety of our children. Should this data be stolen, we will be potentially giving molesters, stalkers, kidnappers, etc. the information to 'lure' our children. Even the best-behaved child can be tempted when you know what their 'weakness' is.

Additionally, there are concerns about the 'underbellies' of the algorithms, which can lead children to suspicious places. For example, my younger brother was in his early tweens when he was watching YouTube and after watching about 6 of the recommended videos (recommended by the algorithm), he started seeing videos that were sexually suggestive. While the content was not explicit, it did make us wonder what other dangers children could be lured into through paid ads, clickbait links, and suggestive videos. Not only should children be monitored when on any online platform, but policies should address the use of children's data from social media platforms. Although many social media platforms have age restrictions, these are easily bypassed.

Lastly, when dealing with children, there are other risks of introducing children to a world that is run by AI. AI makes things easier for us but, in doing so, it can prevent children from learning valuable lessons through trial and error. These skills include social skills and opportunities that they would learn about through a natural conversation with another person. When AI gets involved, the 'smart' predictions can make the child lazy to write themselves, thus proving detrimental for when they have to compose a text by themselves without the help of AI.

Societal issues

Unfortunately, algorithms have a way of amplifying the biases that are present in society. According to

Meltwater CEO, Jorn Lyseggen, "AI is fundamentally biased in how it was created, trained, programmed," (2018) and he worries that people will rely on AI too much. As much as AI is going to influence our decision-making processes, we need to make sure that we are aware of the potential biases that an algorithm could show. An example of algorithmic bias can be found in Amazon's now discontinued recruiting algorithm because it displayed gender bias.

While it may seem that these biases are arbitrary in the world of social media — when the world of social media is connected to reality, it can be detrimental. That even algorithms can be biased shows that the human element will always be needed to balance AI. As much as AI can assist and even improve upon the work that humans can do, it does not possess the same depth of intelligence and ability to adapt that a human does. It lacks the ability to understand the finer nuances of navigating through life.

Policies

AI is expanding at a rapid rate and is expected to flourish for a long time to come. At the moment, governments are not regulating the creation or use of AI and Big Data systems which means that a person can potentially create dangerous technology without a lot of repercussions. There are no policies governing AI because AI is progressing too quickly for government institutions and corporations to create clear, specific, and binding policies. There's no exact path that AI will or can take because there are just infinite possibilities. Which forces you to wonder just how safe it is to be using artificial intelligence technology that is not regulated.

A lack of regulations can mean that corporations can internally 'regulate' their AI systems and send them out into the public. Most people don't read terms of service and could be unwittingly selling their souls. Thankfully, there are groups that are attempting to provide policies and update them as needed.

Advocacy Groups

As noted previously, there are hardly any policies that regulate the use and creation of AI. So, the way to address these ethical concerns is to ensure that there are organizations that will ask these questions. One of the solutions to this is to create policies that govern how AI technology, along with Big Data, are managed, sourced, and used. Thankfully, amidst all of these concerns, there are advocacy groups that can help regulate AI and its use. Some of them include:

Partnership on AI, which is a combined effort between Apple, Amazon, IBM, Facebook, and Microsoft to ensure that people actually understand what AI technologies are and provide the best way to deal with challenges and opportunities brought on by the use of AI and Big Data.

AI Now is a research center that aims at ensuring AI is developed for problems that need solutions instead of merely for fun and games. It also aids in producing 'interdisciplinary research on the social implications of artificial intelligence and acts as a hub for the emerging field focused on these issues" (AI Now, n.d.). AI is progressing at an astounding rate and there should be people or organizations that can regulate it.

In summary

We have looked at the relationship between Big Data and AI. In a nutshell, the two are in a reciprocal relationship where they work with and for each other. Big Data cannot be analyzed without AI's algorithms, and AI cannot be effectively trained without Big Data. This symbiotic relationship allows for AI and Big Data to be integrated into our daily lives effectively and easily. Further than that, we also considered the various industries where you can see these systems in action, as well as how they are benefiting from it. While there are many ethical concerns, the use of AI and Big Data has a lot of potential benefits for everyone involved. The possibility for positive influence is huge, but the possibility for negative influence is just as big. To provide you with a balanced overview we also looked at the possible future of Big Data and AI and a few of the major ethical issues that arise when dealing with this technology.

Conclusion

I hope that this book was as enjoyable for you to read as it was for me to put together! The world of artificial intelligence and Big Data is exciting because there are so many possibilities. But, it can also be scary because there is still a lot of it that is unknown. There is a lot more you can learn about AI that has not been covered in this book. Explaining every component of AI would take forever! In this book, we focused on 3 main concepts: AI, machine learning, and Big Data.

Artificial Intelligence is an attempt to recreate the intelligence of a human. In order to recreate the intelligence of a human, we break it into components: humans have the ability to speak and understand languages, humans can learn new things and adapt, humans are able to move and see. Each of these abilities that a human has can be shown to be translated to one of the components within AI. Understanding different languages falls under Natural Language Processing (NLP) while being able to learn and adapt falls under Machine learning. Humans being able to move and see fall under robotics and computer vision. But, it is only when these abilities can work together in cohesion that we will be able to say that we've successfully recreated intelligence.

Machine learning is a machine that is able to 'learn' things by using algorithms. Although it may seem utterly foreign, humans think and learn quite similarly to machines. After all, machine learning is inspired by human learning. A machine needs an algorithm and data for it to be able to learn — the algorithm is a mathematical expression of what the machine should do and learn, and the data can be likened to prior knowledge or the basics.

When the machine learns, it keeps a log of everything that it's learned and then, through the mathematical process, analyzes the data so that it can 'learn'. You can liken this to learning and then reviewing your notes and remembering (accurately) what was said in class.

As you can see, machine learning was designed with the human thinking and learning process as inspiration. The process that machine learning uses is a lot like the one that you follow at school or when you want to learn something new — there's just a lot less math for you to incorporate. To illustrate: if you want to learn something new, you will need to be taught a few fundamentals (data) so that you can analyze it later and see the correlation between the old information and new information. Machine learning is a sub-discipline of AI. While Big Data is completely different but complementary to AI.

Big Data is a large set of data that cannot be processed through ordinary means. This data is sieved through and an analysis is then provided. For example, the internet is full of raw data that can be used to profile you: everything from how much time you spend online to the average amount of times you click per website will create your profile. This profile can then be used to determine what kind of products you would like to buy, what kind of services you would be interested in, and even what kind of partner you would be compatible with. Fortunately for all of us, everything is not yet being analyzed as we currently lack the computing power to do that.

When AI and Big Data work together, there is an endless list of good things that it could achieve and an equally long list for all the bad things it could be used for. In reading this book, I hope that I have managed to clear some of the misconceptions you may have had about AI, machine learning, and Big Data analytics. In clearing these misconceptions and also providing you with the possible downfalls of integrating them into our lives, I trust that you will be able to create your own understanding of what the integration of these systems means. Lastly, I hope that your interest was piqued because the beauty of AI and Data analytics lies in its utter vastness. Although I have tried to encapsulate all the important points for a person who is just starting on their journey to learn about AI and Big Data analytics, there is so much more. I trust that you were inspired to learn more about Big Data and artificial intelligence, and perhaps even pursue a career in it.

References

All images found on https://pixabay.com/

A. (2021, March 3). *What is natural language processing?* Introduction to NLP. Algorithmia Blog. https://algorithmia.com/blog/introduction-natural-language-processing-nlp

AI Now. (n.d.). *About AI now.* Retrieved March 21, 2021, from https://ainowinstitute.org/about.html

Ambalina, L. (2020, April 1). *What is the difference between CNN and RNN?* Lionbridge AI. https://lionbridge.ai/articles/difference-between-cnn-and-rnn/#:%7E:text=The%20main%20difference%20between%20CNN,as%20a%20sentence%20for%20example.&text=Whereas%2C%20RNNs%20reuse%20activation%20functions,next%20output%20in%20a%20series.

Armstrong, S. (2014, April 7). SHRDLU, understanding, anthropomorphisation and hindsight bias—LessWrong. LESSWRONG. https://www.lesswrong.com/posts/ecGNCMRQNr9aD38mA/shrdlu-understanding-anthropomorphisation-and-hindsight-bias

Aslam, S. (2021, January 6). Facebook by the numbers: Stats, demographics & fun facts. Omnicore. https://www.omnicoreagency.com/facebook-statistics/#:%7E:text=350%20million%20photos%20are%20uploaded,4%2C000%20photo%20uploads%20per%20second.

Baidu. (2021, February 24). These five AI developments will shape 2021 and beyond. MIT Technology Review. https://www.technologyreview.com/2021/01/14/1016122/these-five-ai-developments-will-shape-2021-and-beyond/

Britannica. (n.d.). Artificial intelligence—alan turing and the beginning of AI. Encyclopedia Britannica. Retrieved March 6, 2021, from https://www.britannica.com/technology/artificial-intelligence/Alan-Turing-and-the-beginning-of-AI

Columbus, L. (2018, March 13). *10 ways machine learning is revolutionizing manufacturing in 2018.* Forbes. https://www.forbes.com/sites/louiscolumbus/2018/03/11/10-ways-machine-learning-is-revolutionizing-manufacturing-in-2018/?sh=63dbc8e623ac

CrashCourse. (2019, October 18). Symbolic AI: Crash course AI #10 [Video]. YouTube. https://www.youtube.com/watch?v=WHC04m2VOws&t=136s

Data warehouse manager salary | PayScale. (n.d.). PayScale. Retrieved March 8, 2021, from https://www.payscale.com/research/US/Job=Data_Warehouse_Manager/Salary

Database manager job description. (2018, January 1). JobHero. https://www.jobhero.com/job-description/examples/data-systems-administration/database-manager#:%7E:text=Database%20Managers%20are%20primarily%20responsible,with%20new%20systems%20as%20needed.

Dickson, B. (2018, December 27). The biggest artificial intelligence developments of 2018. TechTalks. https://bdtechtalks.com/2018/12/28/top-artificial-intelligence-stories-2018/

Donges, N. (2020, September 3). A complete guide to the random forest algorithm. Built In. https://builtin.com/data-science/random-forest-algorithm

Editors, Forbes Technology Council. (2018, March 1). 14 ways AI will benefit or harm society. Forbes. https://www.forbes.com/sites/forbestechcouncil/2018/03/01/14-ways-ai-will-benefit-or-harm-society/?sh=37a0b01c4ef0

Expert.ai. (2021, February 11). Natural language understanding: What is it and how is it different from NLP? https://www.expert.ai/blog/natural-language-understanding-different-nlp/

Faggella, D. (2020, April 11). Everyday examples of artificial intelligence and machine learning. Emerj. https://emerj.com/ai-sector-overviews/everyday-examples-of-ai/

Gil Press. (2016, December 30). A very short history of artificial intelligence (AI). Forbes. https://www.forbes.com/sites/gilpress/2016/12/30/a-very-short-history-of-artificial-intelligence-ai/?sh=6f81dff76fba

Greenbird. (2020, June 19). *7 ground-breaking machine learning applications for utilities*. Smart Energy International. https://www.smart-energy.com/industry-sectors/digitalisation/7-ground-breaking-machine-learning-applications-for-utilities/

Guerrouj, L. (2020, June 17). Machine learning: 6 Real-World examples. Salesforce EMEA Blog. https://www.salesforce.com/eu/blog/2020/06/real-world-examples-of-machine-learning.html

Hanson Robotics Limited. (2020, September 1). Sophia. Hanson Robotics. https://www.hansonrobotics.com/sophia/

IBM. (n.d.-a). Big Data analytics. South Africa | IBM. Retrieved March 6, 2021, from https://www.ibm.com/za-en/analytics/hadoop/big-data-analytics

IBM. (n.d.–b). IBM100—deep blue. IBM100. Retrieved March 6, 2021, from https://www.ibm.com/ibm/history/ibm100/us/en/icons/deepblue/transform/

IBM. (n.d.–c). IBM100—the punched card tabulator. IBM100. Retrieved March 7, 2021, from https://www.ibm.com/ibm/history/ibm100/us/en/icons/tabulator/

IBM Cloud Education. (2020a, September 3). Speech recognition. IBM. https://www.ibm.com/cloud/learn/speech-recognition#:%7E:text=Speech%20recognition%2C%20also%20known%20as,speech%20into%20a%20written%20format.&text=IBM%20has%20had%20a%20prominent,of%20%E2%80%9CShoebox%E2%80%9D%20in%201962.

IBM Cloud Education. (2020b, December 18). Machine learning. IBM. https://www.ibm.com/cloud/learn/machine-learning

ImageNet. (n.d.). About ImageNet. Retrieved March 6, 2021, from http://image-net.org/about

Iota Communications, Inc. (2020, November 25). The evolution of IoT sensor data (& how it benefits you) | iota. https://www.iotacommunications.com/blog/iot-sensor-data/

Jha, M. S. (2021, March 2). 15 proven facts why artificial intelligence will create more jobs in 2021. GreatLearning Blog: Free Resources What Matters to Shape Your Career! https://www.mygreatlearning.com/blog/15-reasons-why-ai-will-create-more-jobs-than-it-takes/#:%7E:text=AI%20will%20Create%20one w%20Job,demand%20for%20new%20job%20 positions.

Jones, T. (2017, September 18). The languages of AI. IBM Developer. https://developer.ibm.com/technologies/artificial-intelligence/articles/cc-languages-artificial-intelligence/

Joshi, N. (2020, January 9). How AI and robotics can change taxation. Forbes. https://www.forbes.com/sites/cognitiveworld/2020/01/09/how-ai-and-robotics-can-change-taxation/?sh=609702b46437

Khvoynitskaya, B. S. (2020, December 5). The future of Big Data: 5 predictions from experts for 2020-2025. Itransition. https://www.itransition.com/blog/the-future-of-big-data

Lighthill, J. (1972, July). Lighthill report. Computing at Chilton. http://www.chilton-computing.org.uk/inf/literature/reports/lighthill_report/p001.htm

Marr, B. (2018, December 12). 27 incredible examples of AI and machine learning in practice. Forbes. https://www.forbes.com/sites/bernardmarr/2018/04/30/27-incredible-examples-of-ai-and-machine-learning-in-practice/?sh=77f236177502

Martinez, E. (2019, April 4). SNARC. History of AI. https://historyof.ai/snarc/#:%7E:text=SNARC%20Exhibit%20Label&text=Using%20analog%20and%20electromechanical%20components,)%20for%20long%2Dterm%20memory.

McCarthy, J. (2006, October 30). The dartmouth workshop--as planned and as it happened. Stanford Formal Reasoning Group. http://www-formal.stanford.edu/jmc/slides/dartmouth/dartmouth/node1.html

McCarthy, J., Minsky, M. L., Rochester, N., & Shannon, C. E. (1955, August 31). A PROPOSAL FOR THE DARTMOUTH SUMMER RESEARCH PROJECT ON ARTIFICIAL INTELLIGENCE. Stanford Formal Reasoning Group. http://www-formal.stanford.edu/jmc/history/dartmouth/dartmouth.html

Moné, L. (2020, September 10). Artificial intelligence—expert systems. LeanIX. https://www.leanix.net/en/blog/artificial-intelligence-expert-systems#:%7E:text=In%20artificial%20intelligence%2C%20an%20expert,than%20through%20conventional%20procedural%20code.

Monnappa, A. (2021, February 11). Data science vs. Big Data vs. Data analytics [updated]. Simplilearn.Com. https://www.simplilearn.com/data-science-vs-big-data-vs-data-analytics-article

Mukherjee, S. (2018, January 22). Top 10 breakthroughs in Big Data science in 2017. Data Camp. https://www.datacamp.com/community/blog/breakthroughs-big-data-science-2017

N. (2018, July 29). Rosenblatt's perceptron—pearson education .ORGANIZATION OF THE CHAPTER the perceptron occupies. Vdocuments.Mx. https://vdocuments.mx/rosenblatts-perceptron-pearson-education-organization-of-the-chapter-the.html

Neelakandan, N. (2019, October 18). 5 benefits of machine learning in eLearning. ELearning Industry.

https://elearningindustry.com/machine-learning-benefits-elearning

New Atlas. (2015, June 18). Fifty years of shakey, the "world's first electronic person." https://newatlas.com/shakey-robot-sri-fiftieth-anniversary/37668/#:%7E:text=Shakey%20was%20described%20in%20Life,the%20strength%20of%20Shakey's%20performance.

Nicholson, C. (n.d.). Symbolic reasoning (symbolic AI) and machine learning. Pathmind. Retrieved March 5, 2021, from https://wiki.pathmind.com/symbolic-reasoning

Olavsrud, T. (2020, October 20). What is a data architect? IT's data framework visionary. CIO. https://www.cio.com/article/3586138/what-is-a-data-architect-its-data-framework-visionary.html

OpenAI. (2020, September 2). *Dota 2.* *https://openai.com/blog/dota-2/*

Oracle. (n.d.). Big Data defined. Retrieved March 7, 2021, from https://www.oracle.com/za/big-data/what-is-big-data/

Outside Insight. (2018, November 23). Ethics and transparency in the age of Big Data. https://outsideinsight.com/insights/ethics-and-transparency-in-the-age-of-big-data/

Pedamkar, P. (2021, March 1). Big Data vs machine learning. EDUCBA. https://www.educba.com/big-data-vs-machine-learning/

Picchi, A. (2018, April 25). OK, you've deleted facebook, but is your data still out there? CBS News. https://www.cbsnews.com/news/ok-youve-deleted-facebook-but-is-your-data-still-out-there/

Polly. (2020, March 10). How AI affects the robotics industry and what the future holds. Robotics & Automation News. https://roboticsandautomationnews.com/2020/03/10/how-ai-affects-the-robotic-industry-and-what-the-future-holds/31197/#:%7E:text=In%20the%20future%20AI%20powered,are%20set%20to%20change%20humanity.&text=Robots%20of%20the%20future%20will,radioactive%20substances%20or%20disabling%20bombs.

Raj Ramesh. (2017a, January 21). How to be ready for jobs in an artificial intelligence driven world [Video]. YouTube. https://www.youtube.com/watch?v=gJRVh68P47Y&list=PLrqR8N_AZgNT0jLTsSnxk8URiqs-Sbrzv&index=4

Raj Ramesh. (2017b, August 13). YouTube [Video]. What Is Artificial Intelligence? In 5 Minutes.

https://www.youtube.com/watch?v=2ePf9rue1
Ao&feature=youtu.be

Ray, T. (2021, January 20). Natural language processing (NLP) jobs, salaries, skills, learning path & online courses. | Personalized Career Guidance & Counseling for UG, PG, MBA Programs in USA, UK and Canada | Stoodnt. https://www.stoodnt.com/blog/natural-language-processing-nlp-jobs-salaries-skills-learning-path-online-courses/#NLP_Demand_and_Job_Market

Richman, D. (2016, October 20). Q&A: Uber's machine learning chief says pattern-finding computing fuels ride-hailing giant. GeekWire. https://www.geekwire.com/2016/uber-collapse-without-pattern-finding-computers-says-chief-machine-learning/

Rijmenam, M. (2021, January 21). A short history of Big Data | Experfy.com. Experfy Insights. https://www.experfy.com/blog/bigdata-cloud/a-short-history-of-big-data/

Rose, S. (2020, March 22). What is the future of machine learning?—codeburst. Medium. https://codeburst.io/what-is-the-future-of-machine-learning-f93749833645

Roy, P. (2021, January 19). 13 examples of machine learning applications in real world. Make Informed Upskilling Decisions.

https://learning.naukri.com/articles/13-examples-of-machine-learning-applications-in-real-world/

SAS Analytics. (n.d.). Machine learning: What it is and why it matters. SAS. Retrieved March 12, 2021, from https://www.sas.com/en_us/insights/analytics/machine-learning.html

Sharma, S. (2019, October 11). What the hell is perceptron?—towards data science. Medium. https://towardsdatascience.com/what-the-hell-is-perceptron-626217814f53

Simplilearn. (2021, February 12). What is Big Data analytics and why it is important? Simplilearn.Com. https://www.simplilearn.com/what-is-big-data-analytics-article

Singhal, M. (2020, October 18). Machine learning: Decision trees example in real life. Numpy Ninja. https://www.numpyninja.com/post/decision-trees-example-in-machine-learning

Sood, D. (2019, September 24). Backpropagation concept explained in 5 levels of difficulty. Medium. https://medium.com/coinmonks/backpropaga

tion-concept-explained-in-5-levels-of-difficulty-8b220a939db5

SRI International. (2020, December 21). 75 years of innovation: Shakey the robot—the dish. Medium. https://medium.com/dish/75-years-of-innovation-shakey-the-robot-385af2311ec8

Srinivasan, K. (2020, March 27). Apriori algorithms and their importance in data mining. Digital Vidya. https://www.digitalvidya.com/blog/apriori-algorithms-in-data-mining/

StartUs Insights. (2019, March 5). 5 top Big Data & machine learning startups in energy. https://www.startus-insights.com/innovators-guide/5-top-big-data-machine-learning-startups-in-energy/

TEDx Talks. (2017, April 19). How Big Data can influence decisions that actually matter | prukalpa sankar | TEDxGateway. YouTube. https://www.youtube.com/watch?v=C6WKt6fJiso&feature=youtu.be

Times, T. N. Y. (1988, August 16). Learning, then talking. The New York Times. https://www.nytimes.com/1988/08/16/science/learning-then-talking.html

Toptal. (n.d.). Big Data engineer job description template | toptal®. Retrieved March 8, 2021, from https://www.toptal.com/big-data/job-description#:%7E:text=A%20Big%20Data%20Engineer%20is,vast%20amounts%20of%20data%20quickly.&text=The%20actual%20definiti on%20of%20this,with%20the%20Data%20Sci entist%20role.

Vadapalli, P. (2020, December 22). Random forest vs decision tree: Difference between random forest and decision tree. UpGrad Blog. https://www.upgrad.com/blog/random-forest-vs-decision-tree/#:%7E:text=Decision%20trees%20are%2 0very%20easy,sets%2C%20especially%20the%20linear%20one.

VandeWettering, M. (2011, August 28). Donald michie, alan turing, martin gardner, and tic tac toe – brainwagon. Brainwagon.Org. https://brainwagon.org/2011/08/28/donald-michie-alan-turing-martin-gardner-and-tic-tac-toe/

Vincent, J. (2016, March 24). Twitter taught microsoft's AI chatbot to be a racist asshole in less than a day. The Verge. https://www.theverge.com/2016/3/24/112970 50/tay-microsoft-chatbot-racist

Walker, T. (2018, May 14). Diagnostic analytics 101: Why did it happen? IBM Business Analytics Blog. https://www.ibm.com/blogs/business-analytics/diagnostic-analytics-101-why-did-it-happen/

White, S. K. (2019, April 9). What is a business intelligence analyst? A role for driving business value with data. CIO. https://www.cio.com/article/3387619/what-is-a-business-intelligence-analyst-a-role-for-driving-business-value-with-data.html#:%7E:text=Business%20intelligence%20(BI)%20analysts%20transform,insights%20that%20drive%20business%20value.&text=This%20is%20done%20by%20mining,to%20others%20in%20the%20organization.

Wikipedia contributors. (2020a, November 26). Timeline of machine learning. Wikipedia. https://en.wikipedia.org/wiki/Timeline_of_machine_learning

Wikipedia contributors. (2020b, December 15). Arthur samuel. Wikipedia. https://en.wikipedia.org/wiki/Arthur_Samuel

Wikipedia contributors. (2020c, December 28). SHRDLU. Wikipedia. https://en.wikipedia.org/wiki/SHRDLU

Wikipedia contributors. (2020d, December 31). TD-Gammon. Wikipedia. https://en.wikipedia.org/wiki/TD-Gammon

Wikipedia contributors. (2021a, January 25). Netflix prize. Wikipedia. https://en.wikipedia.org/wiki/Netflix_Prize

Wikipedia contributors. (2021b, January 27). NETtalk (artificial neural network). Wikipedia. https://en.wikipedia.org/wiki/NETtalk_(artificial_neural_network)

Wikipedia contributors. (2021c, February 2). Gartner. Wikipedia. https://en.wikipedia.org/wiki/Gartner

Wikipedia contributors. (2021d, February 13). AIBO. Wikipedia. https://en.wikipedia.org/wiki/AIBO

Wikipedia contributors. (2021e, February 24). Torch (machine learning). Wikipedia. https://en.wikipedia.org/wiki/Torch_(machine_learning)

Wikipedia contributors. (2021f, March 1). ELIZA. Wikipedia. https://en.wikipedia.org/wiki/ELIZA

Wikipedia contributors. (2021g, March 2). Fourth industrial revolution. Wikipedia. https://en.wikipedia.org/wiki/Fourth_Industrial_Revolution

Wikipedia contributors. (2021h, March 3). Alan Turing. Wikipedia. https://en.wikipedia.org/wiki/Alan_Turing

Wikipedia contributors. (2021i, March 5). Perceptron. Wikipedia. https://en.wikipedia.org/wiki/Perceptron

Wikipedia contributors. (2021j, March 8). Principal component analysis. Wikipedia. https://en.wikipedia.org/wiki/Principal_comp onent_analysis#Applications

Willems, K. (2017, November 28). 11 surprising jobs that use data science. Data Camp. https://www.datacamp.com/community/blog/ 11-jobs-data-science

World Economic Forum. (2015, February 25). A brief history of Big Data everyone should read. https://www.weforum.org/agenda/2015/02/a-brief-history-of-big-data-everyone-should-read/

Yadav, R. (2020, December 25). Top 7 artificial intelligence breakthroughs we saw in 2019. Analytics India Magazine. https://analyticsindiamag.com/top-7-artificial-intelligence-breakthroughs-we-saw-in-2019/

Zola, A., & Zola, A. (2020, October 22). Machine learning engineer vs. Data scientist. Springboard Blog. https://www.springboard.com/blog/machine-learning-engineer-vs-data-scientist/#:%7E:text=Machine%20learning%2 0engineers%20feed%20data,terabytes%20of% 20real%2Dtime%20data.

www.ingramcontent.com/pod-product-compliance
Lightning Source LLC
Chambersburg PA
CBHW071250050326
40690CB00011B/2331